MW01048372

THE GOSPEL OF MARK

A Verse-by-Verse Devotional Journey

100 Daily Devotions

from the Bible's Earliest Account

of the Life of Christ

VINCE WILCOX

I dedicate this book to our beloved daughters,
Lauren and Allison.

CONTENTS

PREFACE

E ach time I read the Gospel of Mark, I marvel that something written two thousand years ago can touch me so deeply and change me so profoundly. I'm moved both by the story's hero and its eternal Author.

I hope you will be, too.

I began writing this book in 2009 during my second year of law school. At the beginning of the day, I'd spend time reading Mark and trying to apply the narrative to my own life. I completed the first draft that New Year's Eve. The next year, I had the privilege of leading a small group study of this gospel and incorporated insights from that experience into a revised manuscript. The following year, I taught it again and learned even more; so I continued to revise it. By 2016, I had led four expeditions through Mark, the most recent with an amazing group of single adults at Church of the City in Franklin, Tennessee. I learned so much from my fellow sojourners that I would be ungrateful if I did not thank them for teaching me so much along the way. I also want to thank my friend Mellie Brackett and my brother-in-law Ron Ferguson for helping proof-read this final draft.

I believe that formal theological training is incredibly valuable. I also believe that you don't have to be a distinguished scholar to be a faithful student. Jesus used ordinary men and ordinary words to tell the world about his extraordinary kingdom. As such, I've tried to avoid complicated theological language in this book. My hope is that someone with little religious background--or from any religious background--can read and respond to Mark's revelation of Christ.

I originally organized this book into sixteen chapters corresponding to the traditional chapter divisions of Mark's Gospel. As I taught and re-taught this passage, it seemed more practical to reorganize the material into shorter, chronological episodes based on an incident or topic. That way, the reader's attention could be focused on a short passage and fit the time he or she had available. You have before you a series of 100 devotions of varying lengths. I've concluded each episode with a prayer asking God to apply the truths of that passage to our lives.

At the outset, let me confess that it's a daunting task to craft 100 devotions from a set of verses where every passage has inspired hundreds of thousands of sermons down through the centuries. It's simply impossible to write everything that needs to be said about this gospel or its central character. Looking back, it seemed the more I wrote, the more inadequate I felt. So rather than trying to write an exhaustive (and exhausting) commentary, I hope this simple devotional journal will be helpful to you on your journey.

--*Vince Wilcox*, July 2018

INTRODUCTION

Jesus is the most influential man who ever lived.
More has been spoken, written, and sung about him
than any other person in history. And yet, as his story
makes its way through the filters of time and culture,
much has been lost—if not replaced.

Can we peel back the layers of religion, politics,
and sentimentality to discover Jesus' true mission and
message? Is it possible to shake off our preconceptions
and prejudices and simply experience Jesus as his first
followers did?

Yes. Through the written words of a man named
John Mark.

The New Testament records that Mark was a
cousin of Barnabas, a colleague of the Apostle Paul.
Mark accompanied Paul and Barnabas on missionary
trips and was later mentored by Peter, one of Jesus'
closest disciples. Mark heard Peter preach and teach
extensively about his three years with Christ. He
probably served as Peter's scribe, penning the New
Testament letters the apostle dictated to him.

Detailed narratives of Christ's life and teachings,
called "gospels," began circulating about 30 years after
Jesus' crucifixion. Although there were many such
accounts written by the end of the first century, only
four—the Gospels of Matthew, Mark, Luke and

John—were considered trustworthy enough to be included in the canon of Scripture. Of these four, Mark is thought to be the earliest written. Many scholars believe that Matthew and Luke referenced extensive portions of Mark's Gospel when they wrote their own biographies of Christ.

So how do we know that Mark is accurate? Or for that matter, how can we rely upon the veracity of the entire body of Scripture we call the Bible? This is a crucial question, one whose answer will determine how we think, act, and live.

First, we can acknowledge that eyewitnesses to these events wouldn't have let inaccurate or false testimonies go unchallenged. Second, history records that a significant number of Jesus' immediate followers were martyred for their steadfast insistence upon the truth of these accounts. Would they have died for something they knew to be patently false? Third, believers throughout the centuries have affirmed that Scripture has a God-breathed character that makes it trustworthy and authoritative in our lives. Finally, the fact that the Christian faith continues to grow and is embraced by billions of people two millennia later attests to the power and reliability of this story.

I invite you to dive into the pages of Mark's Gospel with reckless abandon. To resist the temptation to be merely rational or literal or cynical. To find yourself at the bank of the Jordan River and amid the teeming throngs in Jerusalem. To imagine that you are the leper cast out of your community, the parent whose child lay dying, or the bureaucrat offended by Jesus' criticism. Come hungry, desperate, and hurting.

For most of us, this won't take that much imagination.

One last suggestion...

Before you begin this study, take a moment and ask God to reveal himself through the story of his Son, Jesus. For some of us, talking to God might feel awkward and uncomfortable. If so, maybe this will help: if he's not real, then there's nothing to lose. And if he is who he says he is, then you've got everything to gain.

VINCE WILCOX

MARK 1

THE GOSPEL BEGINS

1:1 The beginning of the good news [gospel] about Jesus the Messiah [Christ], the Son of God.

Gospel literally means "good news." It's a word that embodies hope, help, and healing. To Mark, this news is not merely secondhand hearsay or incidental gossip. It's truly the greatest story ever told.

The first phrase out of Mark's pen is *"The beginning."* Every Jew would have recognized these opening words from the first verse of the first book of Hebrew Scripture. Just as the Genesis creation story opens with *"In the beginning God,"* the Gospel of Mark promises to chronicle the story of God's re-creation and redemption of the world.

Mark uses a crisp, no-nonsense approach for his gospel, beginning with the basics: the name, title, and lineage of his hero.

Jesus is a fairly common Jewish name that means "God saves." To Mark and his people, this name is an ever-present plea for the Lord to rescue them from the tyranny of Roman oppression and to fulfill the promises God made to their forefathers. A pagan empire occupies the Promised Land. Naming your child *Jesus* is not only a simple act of faith, it's also a subtle act of rebellion, akin to naming your baby *Abraham Lincoln* if you had been a slave living in the Confederacy during the American Civil War.

"Christ," however, is not a name but a title. It's a Greek word that means the same as the Hebrew word, "Messiah." Greek is the common language of the time, and Mark intentionally pairs a Jewish name, *Jesus*, with a Greek title, *Christ*. First century followers use this hybrid Hebrew/Greek name and title to emphasize that Jesus came to one and all regardless of religion, nationality, politics, gender, or economic status.

The Judean landscape is filled with would-be messiahs: military, political, and religious zealots who promise glory, power, and privilege to their followers. The Romans allow Israel's leaders a fair amount of self-determination as long as they keep their people under control. But punishment is swift and severe if things get the slightest bit out of hand. That's why this "Jesus Movement" particularly alarms the Jewish authorities.

Mark not only presents Jesus' name and title but his lineage as well.

In the Jewish tradition, your father's first name became your legal surname. For example, because my father's first name is "Albert," my legal name would be "Vince, son of Albert." But Mark does something extraordinary here. Rather than simply calling him "Jesus, son of Joseph," Mark refers to him as "Jesus Christ, the Son of God."

Those familiar with the Christmas story know that an angel tells Mary and Joseph that her baby isn't the result of sexual intimacy but rather the miraculous work of the Holy Spirit. The Bible claims that God is Jesus' true father, and Jesus affirms this time and again. When Mark writes that Jesus is the "Son of God," this is precisely what he means. For only the Son of God can do for humanity what it cannot do for itself.

This is truly good news.
The biggest news since the beginning of time.

PRAYER: Heavenly Father, astound me with the goodness of this news! Awe me with the audacity of your Son's coming into occupied territory to rescue me and my world from our captivity. When I speak the name of Jesus, let it be both a cry for deliverance and a declaration that you keep your promises. Help me realize that this story is really your story, written so that the whole world will know a Father's love revealed in the flesh and blood of your Son. Amen.

EPISODE 2

THE FORERUNNER APPEARS

Once Mark introduces his main character, he produces witness after witness to confirm his identity.

> *1:2 as it is written in Isaiah the prophet: "I will send my messenger ahead of you, who will prepare your way"— 3 "a voice of one calling in the wilderness, 'Prepare the way for the Lord, make straight paths for him.' " 4 And so John came, baptizing in the wilderness, preaching a baptism of repentance for the forgiveness of sins.*

In those days, when a king left his palace to venture into his kingdom, he'd have a pretty impressive entourage. Going before him would be a "herald"—an advance man who literally shouted, "The king is coming! Prepare to receive him!" Citizens would line the streets to give the king the honor he was due.

Jewish prophecy declared that the royal Son of God, the Messiah, would also have a forerunner who would prepare the hearts of the people for his arrival. But rather than calling for a parade, this messenger would call for repentance.

Mark identifies John "the Baptizer" as the herald foretold by the prophet Isaiah. John is Jesus' cousin, the son of Mary's sister, Elizabeth, the elderly and childless wife of Zechariah, a humble temple priest. The miraculous birth of John would have reminded every Middle Easterner of God's faithfulness in giving Abraham and Sarah a son in their extreme old age. Abraham is not only the patriarch of the Jews but of the Arabs as well. From the barren wombs of Sarah and Elizabeth, God fulfills his promise to create and redeem his people.

And so John the Baptizer appears in the desert wilderness at the outskirts of Israel's capital city, preaching a message that pierces the hearts of the people.

5 The whole Judean countryside and all the people of Jerusalem went out to him. Confessing their sins, they were baptized by him in the Jordan River. 6 John wore clothing made of camel's hair, with a leather belt around his waist, and he ate locusts and wild honey.

Not much has changed in 2000 years.

In the heart of Israel, ordinary people realize they have missed the mark in their relationship with God and with others. They desperately want to renounce their brokenness and move toward the life their hearts tell them is possible. Even though these people live just a few miles from the epicenter of Jewish worship, the Temple at Jerusalem, their religion is unable to transform and deliver them. So they turn their backs on established religion and walk out into the countryside to hear someone who looks, speaks, and lives like no one they've ever known.

PRAYER: Heavenly Father, help me to realize that my attempt to be "good enough for God" is pointless. Even your chosen people, the Jews, turned a relationship with you into an oppressive religion of rules and regulations. That's what humans do. But you sent your royal Son into the realm to show that you love us nonetheless and that the ache we feel in our hearts is the God-shaped hole that only you can fill. Help me confess both my unrighteousness and self-righteousness and accept your free gift of Christ-righteousness. Amen.

EPISODE 3

JOHN BAPTIZES JESUS

Even as John is receiving their confessions and then symbolically washing them clean in the Jordan River, he is telling them that God is about to do something far more powerful, more permanent, and more personal than anything they have ever known.

> *1:7 And this was his message: "After me comes the one more powerful than I, the straps of whose sandals I am not worthy to stoop down and untie. 8 I baptize you with water, but he will baptize you with the Holy Spirit."*

A sign points the way.

John understands that his calling is to simply point the way to Jesus. Nothing else matters. Not clothes or food or wealth or popularity. John's mission is to "signal" Jesus to his generation.

While a sign points toward something, a symbol actually represents something greater than itself.

America's flag is a symbol. The stars stand for 50 individual states organized into one united whole. The thirteen horizontal stripes symbolize the original number of American colonies; with the red ones representing the blood shed for its freedom and the white ones representing the purity of the principles upon which it was founded. So when soldiers salute the flag or lay down their lives in its defense, they are honoring something far greater than tri-colored cloth.

Likewise, baptism is a symbol.

To the Jews, passing through the water recalls the miraculous deliverance of their people through the Red Sea and the annihilation of Pharaoh's army in its waters. Baptism represents passing from certain death to divine life. It symbolizes the washing away of sins and spiritual purification. It's a public renunciation of selfishness and a public commitment to living for God and others.

More than merely "an outward sign of an inward change," baptism is a profoundly spiritual symbol. Dying to self. Living for God. Rejecting all else. Never turning back.

9 At that time Jesus came from Nazareth in Galilee and was baptized by John in the Jordan.

On this particular morning, I imagine thirty-year-old Jesus hearing his heavenly Father saying something like:

Today is the day.
Tomorrow, nothing will be the same.
Leave your family, your neighbors, and your livelihood as a carpenter.
Go out to where your cousin John is preaching and be baptized.
Stand there in the water, not as a sinner in need of salvation,

*but as a Moses leading my people from slavery to freedom, from
death to life, from sinfulness to holiness.
Your public ministry begins now.
And not only will John be your herald,
but I will personally announce your coming.*

> *10 Just as Jesus was coming up out of the water, he
> saw heaven being torn open and the Spirit descending
> on him like a dove. 11 And a voice came from heaven:
> "You are my Son, whom I love; with you I am well
> pleased."*

In this moment, the Lord of heaven personally
testifies to the unique Sonship of Jesus. The Holy
Spirit of God manifests himself in the likeness of a
dove, tearing through the fabric of reality and
empowering Jesus for the journey ahead.

This is a spectacular event in the history of
redemption: the voice of God the Father, the presence
of the Holy Spirit, and humanity of the Son,
converging in a single time and place.

*PRAYER: Heavenly Father, give me a heart like John the
Baptizer. Let my life point wholly and humbly to the person of
Jesus Christ. Help me understand and confess the depth of my
brokenness and emptiness apart from you. I repent of lifeless
religion and vain self-righteousness. Plunge me daily into the deep
waters of your forgiveness. Wash away my stains and sanctify me
with your goodness. Baptize me not only with water, but also
with your Holy Spirit—who fills me with the love and power I
need to live a life pleasing to you. Amen.*

EPISODE 4

SATAN TEMPTS CHRIST

This transcendent moment at the Jordan doesn't linger. There's a mission to accomplish, and the Holy Spirit of God leads Jesus back out into the wilderness to prepare him for what lies ahead.

> *1:12 At once the Spirit sent him out into the wilderness, 13 and he was in the wilderness forty days, being tempted by Satan. He was with the wild animals, and angels attended him.*

At what point does Satan begin to realize who Jesus really is? Does he overhear Elizabeth and Mary talking about their miraculous pregnancies? Does he cower in the Bethlehem hills as the angels announce the birth of Christ to the shepherds? Do his demons report the 12-year-old spiritual prodigy discussing theology with the elders at the Temple? Does Satan mingle with those standing on the banks of the Jordan River as the heavens tear open and the voice of God shakes the air?

There at the water's edge, the Devil's doubts are washed away as God himself makes it crystal clear that this carpenter's son is the Creator's Son. So the call goes out for every demonic spirit to converge upon this battlefield. Wherever Jesus walks, Satan and his legions will be one step behind. Demonic activity will be unprecedented. Temptation, oppression, and possession will be the order of the day.

And so it begins.

Eons earlier, another man faced the very first temptation. Surrounded by the animals he had helped name, Adam's hunger for the forbidden fruit and his desire to be his own god caused him to break faith with his Creator.

Jesus—the "new Adam"—now undergoes his own temptation on behalf of humanity. Satan's temptations are subtle, yet lethal, testing a physically hungry and spiritually vulnerable Messiah for weeks on end. But rather than falling prey to Lucifer's lies, Christ keeps faith with his Father and prepares to take the battlefield himself.

14 After John was put in prison, Jesus went into Galilee, proclaiming the good news of God. 15 "The time has come," he said. "The kingdom of God has come near. Repent and believe the good news!"

Like the proverbial baseball umpire, John "calls 'em like he sees 'em." So when this prophet raises his voice in outrage that the regional governor and his new wife have both shamelessly divorced their former spouses to marry one another, John the Baptist is thrown in prison.

Jesus returns from his ordeal in the wilderness and picks up preaching where John has left off. But there is one critical difference: Jesus is not just the messenger.

He is the message himself.
   The time has come.

PRAYER: Heavenly Father, help me take Satan seriously. Help me recognize and reject the Tempter's voice. Help me despise what sin does to my heart and to the hearts of those around me. Help me lean on you like your Son did when he was tempted. Empower me by your Spirit to take my sword and shield onto the battlefield to liberate those who have been taken captive. Let me look to that day when Satan will be ultimately destroyed and eternally vanquished from this war zone in which we temporarily live. For the kingdom and the power and the glory belong to you and you alone. Amen.

HIS IRRESISTIBLE INVITATION

1:16 As Jesus walked beside the Sea of Galilee, he saw Simon and his brother Andrew casting a net into the lake, for they were fishermen. 17 "Come, follow me," Jesus said, "and I will send you out to fish for people." 18 At once they left their nets and followed him. 19 When he had gone a little farther, he saw James son of Zebedee and his brother John in a boat, preparing their nets. 20 Without delay he called them, and they left their father Zebedee in the boat with the hired men and followed him.

To the casual observer, Jesus is just another Jewish "rabbi"—a spiritual teacher. A rabbi would call the brightest and the best students around him to learn his "yoke," his interpretive point of view, so that it could be passed along to the faithful.

But rather than painstakingly interviewing the brightest and the best, Jesus goes to the seashore and asks two sets of fishermen brothers to join him. Though Jesus' reputation no doubt precedes him, these men literally drop what they're doing, leave life as they know it, and become his disciples.

Mark writes that Simon, Andrew, James and John follow Christ "at once" and "without delay."

Even the way Jesus calls them is remarkable.

His invitation appeals to their core passions: in this case, fishing. There's a winsome, joyful irony to Christ's call. It's if he is saying, *"You thought you were born to fish; let me show you what real fishing is all about. It's not about scales and fins—it's about hearts and souls!"*

Most of us would weigh risk and reward, cost against benefit, and upside versus downside. I would deliberate, hesitate, and vacillate. But to these men, the call is so clear and compelling that no other option seems possible.

At this moment, saying "no" to Jesus is unimaginable.

PRAYER: Heavenly Father, help me hear the irresistible call of Christ to come and follow. Help me understand that this call isn't to destroy my deepest desires but rather to fulfill them. Let me drop my nets and abandon everything today to follow him. When I am insecure, looking for a "safety net" backup plan, give me the faith to believe there's no safer place than in your Son's company, walking beside him on the road of life. Amen.

EPISODE 6

AMAZED BY HIS AUTHORITY

1:21 They went to Capernaum, and when the Sabbath came, Jesus went into the synagogue and began to teach. 22 The people were amazed at his teaching, because he taught them as one who had authority, not as the teachers of the law.

While there is only one Temple in Israel, many towns have their own synagogue. The synagogue is the center of Jewish religious and cultural life. It is a place of prayer, worship, and schooling.

On this particular Sabbath, Jesus enters the synagogue in Capernaum, the seaside village home of the four fishermen who have just become his disciples. Jesus teaches with such authority that the people are astounded. He speaks as one who has firsthand knowledge of the Truth.

But the brightness of this moment is broken by a dark presence.

23 Just then a man in their synagogue who was possessed by an impure spirit cried out, 24 "What do you want with us, Jesus of Nazareth? Have you come to destroy us? I know who you are—the Holy One of God!" 25 "Be quiet!" said Jesus sternly. "Come out of him!" 26 The impure spirit shook the man violently and came out of him with a shriek. 27 The people were all so amazed that they asked each other, "What is this? A new teaching—and with authority! He even gives orders to impure spirits and they obey him."

Mark writes that a man in the synagogue possessed by an evil spirit shouts out something like, "Jesus, we know who you are and what you've come to do!" Christ shuts up the demonic force and dramatically delivers the man from his spiritual bondage.

28 News about him spread quickly over the whole region of Galilee. 29 As soon as they left the synagogue, they went with James and John to the home of Simon and Andrew. 30 Simon's mother-in-law was in bed with a fever, and they immediately told Jesus about her. 31 So he went to her, took her hand and helped her up. The fever left her and she began to wait on them.

The onlookers, who are electrified by Jesus' powerful preaching, are now beside themselves because of the authority he demonstrates over spiritual forces. But the story doesn't end there. Jesus and his disciples leave the synagogue and go to the home of Simon and Andrew, where their mother is gravely ill with a fever.

Jesus heals her.

In these few verses, Jesus clearly establishes his

lordship over the mind, the spirit, and the body.

> *32 That evening after sunset the people brought to Jesus all the sick and demon-possessed. 33 The whole town gathered at the door, 34 and Jesus healed many who had various diseases. He also drove out many demons, but he would not let the demons speak because they knew who he was.*

The Jewish day starts at sunset, echoing the creation narrative where the darkness precedes the light. So after the Sabbath has ended and the prohibition against work and travel has expired, virtually the whole town shows up at the door of the house where Christ is staying.

Jesus heals and delivers because his Father's children are sick and oppressed.

Word spreads like wildfire.
The long awaited Messiah is in their midst.

PRAYER: Jesus, let me be utterly amazed by your authority over every aspect of my life. Though you have ransomed me from my sin and are the rightful owner of all that I am, you beckon me to bow my knee and give my heart to you in sweet obedience. Only then can you transform my unsound mind, heal my failing body, and deliver my enslaved spirit. Cast out the darkness I so readily entertain. Free me from ungodly habits that have numbed me to your holiness. Create in me a clean heart, O Lord, and renew a right spirit within me. Amen.

EPISODE 7

BEGINNING THE DAY
WITH PRAYER

1:35 Very early in the morning, while it was still dark, Jesus got up, left the house and went off to a solitary place, where he prayed.

If Jesus--the very Son of God--makes it a point to start the day with his heavenly Father, what makes me think I will be effective doing any less?

36 Simon and his companions went to look for him, 37 and when they found him, they exclaimed: "Everyone is looking for you!" 38 Jesus replied, "Let us go somewhere else—to the nearby villages—so I can preach there also. That is why I have come."

Have you ever been so excited by what lay before you that you just couldn't wait to get on with it? Or maybe you've had a taste of something wonderful and couldn't wait to enjoy it again?

I can almost hear the eagerness in Jesus' voice:

Come on, men!
If you thought yesterday was amazing, just wait till today!
There are places to go!
A message to preach!
People to redeem!

PRAYER: Jesus, if I am to be like you, then I must do what you did. You started the day by spending time with your heavenly Father. I imagine you meditated on your Father's Word and prayed for wisdom and strength. More than a blessing before a meal or a desperate plea in an emergency, your prayers bathed the coming day with power from above. You anticipated your Father's powerful hand opening each door and empowering each encounter. As each hour rolled out, you saw your prayers answered as your Father's will was done on earth as it is in heaven. I want what you had, so help me do what you did. Amen!

EPISODE 8

CLEANSING A MAN
WITH LEPROSY

1:39 So he traveled throughout Galilee, preaching in their synagogues and driving out demons. 40 A man with leprosy came to him and begged him on his knees, "If you are willing, you can make me clean."

Leprosy was not only a physical condition; it was a spiritual and social sickness as well. Victims of this devastating disease were shunned from their families and synagogues and forced to live on the edges of society. To even touch a leper was to be made "unclean." As such, this man wasn't asking for a healing as much as he was begging for a cleansing.

41 Jesus was indignant. He reached out his hand and touched the man. "I am willing," he said. "Be clean!" 42 Immediately the leprosy left him and he was cleansed. 43 Jesus sent him away at once with a strong warning: 44 "See that you don't tell this to anyone. But go, show yourself to the priest and offer the sacrifices that Moses commanded for your cleansing, as a testimony to them."

Even though touching a leper will make him ceremonially unclean, Jesus' heart is broken for the plight of this man. Christ reaches out his hand to heal him, and the man is instantly cured from the disease that ravages his body and from the stigma that separates him from his community and church. Jesus instructs him not to publicize this miracle, but rather to present himself—with the proper religious sacrifices—to the very priests who have segregated him.

> *45 Instead he went out and began to talk freely, spreading the news. As a result, Jesus could no longer enter a town openly but stayed outside in lonely places. Yet the people still came to him from everywhere.*

So who is this Jesus?

One by one, John Mark's witnesses step up and testify to the divinity of Jesus: Jewish Scripture, John the Baptist, God the Father, the Holy Spirit, Satan and his demons, Jesus' disciples, a town whose citizens are healed and delivered.

And this is just the beginning.

PRAYER: Jesus, even your family and friends are astounded by what you say and do. Demons are banished. Lepers are cleansed. Fevers are cooled. Nets are abandoned. Prophecy is fulfilled. And yet, I am often lukewarm to your words, unmoved by your miracles, indifferent to the audacity of your incarnation. Rock my world the way you shook those who heard your voice and felt your touch. Change my heart, O God! I'm not just asking... I'm begging. Amen.

MARK 2

EPISODE 9

MEN BRING A PARALYTIC

2:1 A few days later, when Jesus again entered Capernaum, the people heard that he had come home. 2 They gathered in such large numbers that there was no room left, not even outside the door, and he preached the word to them.

Only a short time earlier, Jesus was a relatively obscure rabbi recruiting disciples on the shores of the Sea of Galilee. Now he can barely step into a town without causing a riot. He slips back into Capernaum, but word gets out. A multitude swarms the house where he is staying.

The throng is so thick you can't push your way through. Maybe you've been at a sports event or rock concert where people are literally lifted off the ground or trampled under foot by the dense crowd. It's unnerving, to say the least.

3 Some men came, bringing to him a paralyzed man, carried by four of them.

Imagine this: your friend can't walk, can't provide for himself, or even use the bathroom without assistance. He leads a hopeless, humiliating existence. There are no wheelchair ramps in first century Galilee; there aren't even wheelchairs. Just one despair-filled day after another.

Maybe this man is your son, your brother, or the best man from your wedding. Word reaches you that a rabbi with miraculous healing powers is in your town. You drop whatever you're doing and beg anyone within earshot to grab the corners of the blanket where he lays and bring him to the house where this prophet is preaching.

It is no small feat to carry your paralyzed friend, but hope grows with every step. Rounding the corner, the alleyway is mobbed with those who arrived before you.

> *4 Since they could not get him to Jesus because of the crowd, they made an opening in the roof above Jesus by digging through it and then lowered the mat the man was lying on.*

Undaunted, you push your way around back to the steps that lead up to the roof. Hauling your friend's limp body up the stairs, the four of you take whatever sharp objects you can find and desperately begin digging through the tiles. Jesus stands only a few feet below, and destroying your neighbor's roof seems a small price to pay for your friend's healing. As the opening grows, the people in the room below start pointing up to where you are. Some start to panic, but the burgeoning crowd outside the house prevents those inside from fleeing the falling debris. Finally, the hole is large enough for you to lower your friend down by the corners of his mat.

But rather than simply healing him, Jesus does something even more outrageous.

5 When Jesus saw their faith, he said to the paralyzed man, "Son, your sins are forgiven." 6 Now some teachers of the law were sitting there, thinking to themselves, 7 "Why does this fellow talk like that? He's blaspheming! Who can forgive sins but God alone?"

Instead of helping him walk, Jesus forgives his sins.

You're stunned.

The religious teachers in the room are outraged. "Blasphemer!" they fume. "Only God can forgive sins!"

8 Immediately Jesus knew in his spirit that this was what they were thinking in their hearts, and he said to them, "Why are you thinking these things? 9 Which is easier: to say to this paralyzed man, 'Your sins are forgiven,' or to say, 'Get up, take your mat and walk'? 10 But I want you to know that the Son of Man has authority on earth to forgive sins." So he said to the man, 11 "I tell you, get up, take your mat and go home." 12 He got up, took his mat and walked out in full view of them all. This amazed everyone and they praised God, saying, "We have never seen anything like this!"

Jesus heals the man's infirmity to show that he has the authority to forgive his sins.

The crowd goes wild.

His critics go ballistic.

With Jesus, there's rarely a middle ground.

It's at this encounter where Mark records Jesus calling himself "the Son of Man." The Jewish ear would immediately recognize this as a term for "God's anointed One" that was used by the Old Testament prophets Ezekiel and Daniel.

PRAYER: Jesus, help me realize that my greatest problem isn't physical but spiritual. That my sin—my willful rebellion against your plan and purpose for my life—separates me from God and all he has created me to be. You came, both Son of God and Son of Man, to forgive my sin and heal my brokenness. Thank you for friends and family who were undaunted in their efforts to bring me to you. May I carry the corner of someone else's blanket, bearing them to you so that your grace and power might transform him or her. Amen.

EPISODE 10

THE CALLING OF
LEVI THE TAX COLLECTOR

*2:13 Once again Jesus went out beside the lake. A
large crowd came to him, and he began to teach them.
14 As he walked along, he saw Levi son of Alphaeus
sitting at the tax collector's booth. "Follow me," Jesus
told him, and Levi got up and followed him.*

The crowds grow with his reputation. Jesus and his
disciples return to the Sea of Galilee, which is
actually a very large lake with about 33 miles of
shoreline. Because this is a commercial center, the
Romans have established a tax collection booth here
where Jewish citizens are compelled to pay monetary
tribute to Caesar.

Tax collectors are despised for a number of
reasons. First, they're considered traitors who've sold
out their own people to work for the occupying
Roman Empire. Second, they're notoriously
unscrupulous, often overcharging citizens and keeping
the "skim" for themselves. If the crowds following
Jesus think that he has come to deliver them from the

Romans, they are confused when he stops at the tax collector's booth and calls Levi to be one of his closest followers.

How can Jesus betray his own people? Would the true Messiah invite someone so despicable into his inner circle?

> *15 While Jesus was having dinner at Levi's house, many tax collectors and sinners were eating with him and his disciples, for there were many who followed him. 16 When the teachers of the law who were Pharisees saw him eating with the sinners and tax collectors, they asked his disciples: "Why does he eat with tax collectors and sinners?" 17 On hearing this, Jesus said to them, "It is not the healthy who need a doctor, but the sick. I have not come to call the righteous, but sinners."*

Having taken Levi into his inner circle, Levi wastes no time inviting Christ into his. Perhaps this very same evening, he holds a banquet for Jesus and his fellow tax collectors at his home.

Jesus engages the unrighteous, while outraging the self-righteous.

His most vocal criticism comes from an ultra-conservative sect of Jewish teachers called Pharisees, a name meaning "separated." These men pride themselves on their extremely literal interpretation of Jewish Scripture and the stern, ascetic lifestyle they preach. Their central teaching is that God will deliver and restore Israel only when her people fully obey his commands as they interpret them.

The Pharisees simply can't imagine a Messiah who

consorts with lepers, tax collectors, and prostitutes. Jesus counters that it's precisely the sick that need a physician. He implies that those—especially the self-righteous--who won't acknowledge their own sin-sickness will eventually suffer and die from it. In contrast, those who recognize the severity of their sin are in the presence of a Savior who can readily deliver them.

PRAYER: Lord, although you've commanded us to forgive others the way you've forgiven us, I find myself being stingy with your grace. Even though you've saved me from sins you detest, I doubt your ability to save others whose sins I detest. Deliver me from my self-righteousness, and let me reach out to others the way you reach out to me. Help me see that sin is humanity's disease, that you are the divine cure, and that you are empowering us to be your physicians in a sick and dying world. Amen.

EPISODE 11

FEASTING AND FASTING

2:18 Now John's disciples and the Pharisees were fasting. Some people came and asked Jesus, "How is it that John's disciples and the disciples of the Pharisees are fasting, but yours are not?" 19 Jesus answered, "How can the guests of the bridegroom fast while he is with them? They cannot, so long as they have him with them. 20 But the time will come when the bridegroom will be taken from them, and on that day they will fast."

Jesus doesn't behave the way people think religious leaders should behave. For example, John's disciples and the Pharisees practice the spiritual discipline of fasting--denying the appetites of the body in order to focus on their hunger and thirst for spiritual nourishment.

Jesus doesn't oppose fasting. [We know this because he fasts during his forty days of spiritual preparation in the wilderness.] But when some critics question why his own disciples aren't fasting, he uses this opportunity to reveal something profound about himself.

Jesus responds that one day his followers *will* fast;

but these days, it's as if his disciples are groomsmen celebrating with their honored friend, the bridegroom. People don't fast at a wedding; they feast! Jesus' presence with his disciples is an occasion for joy and revelry.

The analogy of the bride and groom signify much more than just an earthly ritual: they reveal Christ's role as the eternal Groom who has come to pursue his Bride, the Church, for whom he will lay down his life and with whom he will eventually consummate his marriage at the Wedding Feast of the Lamb (Revelation 19:6-9).

PRAYER: Lord, let me realize that spiritual disciplines like fasting and meditation are tools to help me know you more deeply and be transformed by that experience. Only you can truly change me, so repetition and ritual for their own sake mean nothing. When I focus on myself, I do so for selfish and self-glorifying reasons. When I focus on you, you reveal who you are and who I am in you. This difference makes all the difference. One day, I will see you the way you see me. I will be an honored guest at your wedding feast. Let me live in joyful expectation of that day! Amen.

EPISODE 12

WHY A PATCHWORK FAITH FAILS

2:21 "No one sews a patch of unshrunk cloth on an old garment. Otherwise, the new piece will pull away from the old, making the tear worse. 22 And no one pours new wine into old wineskins. Otherwise, the wine will burst the skins, and both the wine and the wineskins will be ruined. No, they pours new wine into new wineskins."

The coming kingdom of God will require a whole new way of thinking and living. Simply taking a new idea and stitching it to an old one will fail them both.

Jesus follows this analogy with a similar illustration: pouring new, unfermented wine into an old, stretched-out wineskin will only result in the old wineskin bursting as the fermentation process expands it.

No, just as new wine requires a new wineskin, the new life of the Spirit will require a new creation to inhabit. Citizens of his kingdom will need more than reformation; they will need rebirth.

Jesus' mission is to redeem the world and

everyone in it. It will cost him his life to achieve it, and it will cost us our lives to receive it. Holding onto our old ways is a futile and ruinous endeavor because Jesus and his Father are making all things new.

PRAYER: Jesus, time and again I find myself trying to marry your kingdom values with my worldly ones--to wedge my square peg of sinfulness into your round whole of holiness. But this is not to be. Life in you is radically different than life without you. My old life was darkness; your new life is light. My old life was filled with pride and anger and lust; your new life is humility and peace and love. Help me take off the old self and put on the new self. Help me hate my garments of shame and love your garments of praise. No compromise, just obedience. Thank you for accepting me "just as I am" but loving me too much to let me stay that way. Renew me. Amen.

EPISODE 13

OBSERVING THE SABBATH

2:23 One Sabbath Jesus was going through the grainfields, and as his disciples walked along, they began to pick some heads of grain. 24 The Pharisees said to him, "Look, why are they doing what is unlawful on the Sabbath?" 25 He answered, "Have you never read what David did when he and his companions were hungry and in need? 26 In the days of Abiathar the high priest, he entered the house of God and ate the consecrated bread, which is lawful only for priests to eat. And he also gave some to his companions." 27 Then he said to them, "The Sabbath was made for man, not man for the Sabbath. 28 So the Son of Man is Lord even of the Sabbath."

To the Jewish nation, keeping the Sabbath was a sacred act that defined them before God and distinguished them from the surrounding pagan nations. It was one of the Ten Commandments the Lord had given Moses: all of Israel was to set aside every seventh day for rest and worship.

So Jewish law prohibited any sort of work. Meals had to be prepared in advance. Firewood was gathered the day before. Ordinances dictated how many steps you could take. Even the smallest infractions were forbidden.

On this particular Sabbath, Jesus and his disciples are walking through a field and begin picking off some heads of wheat to eat. It's unclear whether the grain is from the main body of the crop or from the unharvested edges of the field that the Jews left as provision for the poor.

Whatever the case, the Pharisees (who apparently didn't think it was "work" for them to stalk Jesus as he traveled) take issue. They accuse Jesus and his followers of being Sabbath-breakers who violate God's law and disqualify themselves from God's blessing. The Pharisees are quick to claim Abraham, Moses, and David as their spiritual and ancestral fathers. They quote chapter and verse from the Patriarchs' teachings to justify their own positions and vilify their adversaries.

In response, Jesus tells the Pharisees to consider the story of their beloved King David, who "illegally" ate consecrated bread from the house of God and then gave it to his men to relieve their hunger. Jesus counters that God mandated the Sabbath as a blessing for mankind, not as a curse. He concludes with a startling declaration: "So the Son of Man is Lord even of the Sabbath."

Without pride or pretense, Jesus simply states that the One who gave this command is in their presence. He makes no secret of his claim to divinity and to the authority that comes from being the Son of the Most High God.

PRAYER: Jesus, you are not only Lord of the Sabbath but of every moment of my life. You created all things and rested on the seventh day—not because you were tired--but because you knew we would be. You commanded your people to rest as a witness to your sovereignty and as a provision for our humanity. Deliver me from legalism about observing a day of rest. Likewise, fill me with a desire to set aside work one day a week to honor you with worship, fellowship, and celebration. Amen.

MARK 3

EPISODE 14

HEALING ON THE SABBATH

Jesus doesn't act anything like the Messiah the Jews are expecting.

He enlists the unworthy.

He touches the unclean.

He heals on the Sabbath.

He claims to forgive sins.

He defies his own religious establishment.

In this next set of encounters, Christ will be characterized as a criminal, a demoniac, and a lunatic.

Everyone knows where Jesus will be on the Sabbath. And everyone knows that astonishing things happen wherever he goes. So those in need of healing make sure to get to the synagogue early, as do those who are looking for evidence to accuse Jesus of blasphemy or treason.

> *3:1 Another time Jesus went into the synagogue, and a man with a shriveled hand was there. 2 Some of them were looking for a reason to accuse Jesus, so they watched him closely to see if he would heal him on the*

Sabbath. 3 Jesus said to the man with the shriveled hand, "Stand up in front of everyone."

I imagine this crippled man is either terribly hopeful or hopelessly terrified. Did he come on his own or did others drag him against his will to this showdown?

But Jesus isn't grandstanding. With every eye in the room upon him, he redirects their attention inward to the condition of their own hearts.

4 Then Jesus asked them, "Which is lawful on the Sabbath: to do good or to do evil, to save life or to kill?" But they remained silent.

It's as if he's asking, *"Does the God you serve really prefer legalism over love? Would you actually choose 'keeping the Sabbath' over relieving the suffering of one of God's children? Are your hearts that hard?"*

Instead of repentance, there is only silence.

Jesus is absolutely furious that God's people gathered in God's house on God's day would not speak up for one of God's children who needs hope and healing.

5 He looked around at them in anger and, deeply distressed at their stubborn hearts, said to the man, "Stretch out your hand." He stretched it out, and his hand was completely restored. 6 Then the Pharisees went out and began to plot with the Herodians how they might kill Jesus.

It's ironic that the miracle of this man's healing

49

becomes the incident that marks Jesus for death. The Jewish leaders are outraged by this rabbi's defiance and disrespect. From this day on, the Pharisees will conspire with the supporters of ruler Herod Antipas to bring about Christ's execution.

PRAYER: Jesus, forgive me when I don't stand and speak for those who cannot. Break my heart for the things that break yours. Help me have the courage to be labeled a lunatic for caring more about your children than the letter of the law. Help me understand how profoundly angry and disappointed you are when we misrepresent your love and mercy. Finally, help me become a true agent of healing—a conduit of your grace--to this wounded and weary world. Amen.

EPISODE 15

DEMONIC REALITIES

3:7 Jesus withdrew with his disciples to the lake, and a large crowd from Galilee followed. 8 When they heard all he was doing, many people came to him from Judea, Jerusalem, Idumea, and the regions across the Jordan and around Tyre and Sidon. 9 Because of the crowd he told his disciples to have a small boat ready for him, to keep the people from crowding him. 10 For he had healed many, so that those with diseases were pushing forward to touch him.

The crowds grow even larger and now come from as far away as northern Israel and southern Lebanon. Needless to say, this makes the Pharisees even more fearful that Jesus will upset the delicate religious and political balance they've established with Herod Antipas and the Roman Empire.

But Jesus won't let himself be a pawn in anyone's game. He avoids situations that can get out of control. He often speaks from a small boat moored just offshore, so that the people will not crush against him as he ministers. And if he needs to leave, he can.

Nor will Christ allow demonic spirits to speak out through those they oppress.

11 Whenever the impure spirits saw him, they fell down before him and cried out, "You are the Son of God." 12 But he gave them strict orders not to tell others about him.

This is as good a time as any to talk about spiritual realities. If we believe in an immortal, invisible, and omnipotent God, then it's not difficult to conceive that he has also created a host of other spiritual beings to inhabit his universe.

The Bible records that Satan was once an archangel responsible for the worship of God. Not satisfied with serving, Lucifer rebelled against God and was cast out of heaven, along with the angels who were involved in this futile uprising. While on earth, Satan, in the form of a beautiful serpent, deceived Adam and Eve in Eden and subjected all of Creation to the Fall. Since that time, he and his fallen spirits have conspired in the ongoing destruction of life in our world. But as powerful as the devil and his demons may be, they are still only created beings. God, however, is Creator, and has ordained a plan for redemption that will not only undo the Fall but redeem his children, punish the wicked, and inaugurate a new heaven and new earth where he will reign forever.

This story is more than symbolic—it involves spiritual and physical realities so much bigger than our minds can grasp. In our humanity, we're inclined to only believe what we can see. That's one reason why our "enlightened" Western minds have a hard time accepting the existence of demons.

When Jesus, God's Messiah, begins his ministry,

he confronts demonic reality after demonic reality. These fallen spiritual beings have oppressed, tormented, and enslaved the bodies, minds, and spirits of people for centuries. But Christ has come to set humanity free. He can, he does, and he will.

PRAYER: Heavenly Father, open the eyes of my heart so that I'll not only experience your power and love but that I'll also recognize and rebuke the demonic forces that conspire against you and your children. Help me not to fear the darkness but to bring your light—against which the darkness must flee. At the cross, your Son destroyed sin, death, and the power of hell itself. Then Christ rose to free the possessed, deliver the oppressed, and encourage the depressed. Help me be to others what you are to me. Amen!

EPISODE 16

JESUS COMMISSIONS TWELVE

3:13 Jesus went up on a mountainside and called to him those he wanted, and they came to him. 14 He appointed twelve [designating them apostles] that they might be with him and that he might send them out to preach 15 and to have authority to drive out demons.

The "God Save Us" prayers of humanity are answered in Jesus, who begins building an army of liberators who will crush these spiritual enemies after his ultimate victory on a cross outside of Jerusalem.

In the meantime, we should not be surprised at the frequency or intensity of the spiritual encounters recorded in Mark's Gospel.

16 These are the twelve he appointed: Simon (to whom he gave the name Peter) 17 James son of Zebedee and his brother John (to them he gave the name Boanerges, which means "sons of thunder"); 18 Andrew, Philip, Bartholomew, Matthew, Thomas, James son of Alphaeus, Thaddaeus, Simon the Zealot 19 and Judas Iscariot, who betrayed him.

It's only natural that Mark lists Simon Peter first. After all, many scholars believe that it's Peter who mentors Mark after his conversion.

These core followers are often referred to as the Twelve, the inner circle of men who live with Jesus day in and day out for almost three years. With the exception of Judas Iscariot (who hangs himself after betraying Christ) and John the Beloved (who spends his final years exiled to the island of Patmos) most church historians believe that the other ten apostles were eventually martyred for their faith.

Because the nation of Israel is comprised of twelve tribes, the number twelve has great significance to the Jews. When Jesus calls the Twelve, he's commissioning a "new Israel" who will experience the fulfillment of the covenants God made with Abraham, Isaac, Jacob, and their sons.

PRAYER: Lord, you not only invited these men to follow you, you appointed them as your ambassadors. Even more, you empowered them with your authority to teach, preach, deliver, and heal. It wasn't their calling or appointment or empowerment—it was yours. Lord, let me hear your invitation to come. Let me accept your call to serve. Most of all, give me your power to accomplish all you ask. Without it, I will surely fail. With it, I cannot help but succeed. Amen.

EPISODE 17

JESUS' SANITY AND SPIRITUALITY CHALLENGED

3:20 Then Jesus entered a house, and again a crowd gathered, so that he and his disciples were not even able to eat. 21 When his family heard about this, they went to take charge of him, for they said, "He is out of his mind." 22 And the teachers of the law who came down from Jerusalem said, "He is possessed by Beelzebub! By the prince of demons he is driving out demons."

Jesus' family is planning an intervention. Enough is enough. They've come to take him home so that he might recover from his madness.

The religious authorities that have come down from the capital city aren't as kind in their diagnosis. They acknowledge the miracles, but attribute them to Satan, who—they surmise—must have possessed this carpenter-turned-exorcist.

23 So Jesus called them over to him and began to speak to them in parables: "How can Satan drive out

Satan? 24 If a kingdom is divided against itself, that kingdom cannot stand. 25 If a house is divided against itself, that house cannot stand. 26 And if Satan opposes himself and is divided, he cannot stand; his end has come. 27 In fact, no one can enter a strong man's house [and carry off his possessions] without first tying him up. Then he can plunder the strong man's house.

Again, Jesus uses their own arguments to reveal something more of his nature to them. Christ argues that Satan can't be at cross-purposes with himself. Why would Beelzebub tear down his own kingdom?

Jesus asserts that these miracles prove that someone even stronger than Satan is at work, breaking into his stronghold and disabling him.

Who could that be?

Only the Son of God is powerful enough to overwhelm the dark lord and take back that which rightfully belongs to the Father.

28 Truly I tell you, people can be forgiven all their sins and every slander they utter, 29 But whoever blasphemes against the Holy Spirit will never be forgiven; they are guilty of an eternal sin." 30 He said this because they were saying, "He has an evil spirit."

Over the years, I have heard of some gangs or satanic covens that required their members to "blaspheme the Holy Spirit" and thus commit the "unpardonable sin" as part of their initiation rites. Undeniably, this is a serious offense to God with eternal consequences. But all sin has eternal consequences until we repent and are redeemed. Anyone who can't tell the difference between what God is doing and what Satan is doing is desperately lost. And that includes the religious elite.

The unpardoned sin is the one for which the sinner absolutely refuses to seek forgiveness. It's not unpardonable because God won't forgive; rather, it remains unforgiven because a sinner won't repent.

When we put our faith in Christ, he offers the unshakeable security that comes from knowing that we are forgiven from all our sins—past, present, and future. He replaces our self-righteousness and sin-addiction with a "gospel sanity" that often looks like madness to the world.

PRAYER: Jesus, draw me so close to you that the light of your glory and grace illuminates every part of my life. Expose my subtle compromises and little lies—anything that might chill my heart and numb my spirit to your holiness. Make me aware of my great need so that I might more fully rest in your even greater provision. Re-sensitize me to the reality of the spiritual battlefield on which I live. Help me to hear the call to battle and to take up the spiritual armor you've provided that I might not only resist all of Satan's attacks but also serve on the frontline of your victory. Amen.

EPISODE 18

THE FAMILY REDEFINED

3:31 Then Jesus' mother and brothers arrived. Standing outside, they sent someone in to call him. 32 A crowd was sitting around him, and they told him, "Your mother and brothers are outside looking for you." 33 "Who are my mother and my brothers?" he asked. 34 Then he looked at those seated in a circle around him and said, "Here are my mother and my brothers! 35 Whoever does God's will is my brother and sister and mother."

There's no doubt that Jesus loves his earthly family. From the cross, Christ will look down upon his mother and commit her care to his beloved friend, John the apostle. Years later, James, Jesus' half-brother, will lead the church in Jerusalem.

Family matters to Jesus, so much that he extends that deep circle of intimacy from those who are blood-related to those who will be blood-bought. His Father is God, so anyone who obeys his Father is—by definition—Jesus' brother or sister.

Another time, Jesus will say that anyone who loves persons or property more than he loves Jesus is not fit for the Kingdom (Matthew 10:37). Indeed, he seems to say we must "hate" family and friends—and even ourselves (Luke 14:26). But Christ is not speaking literally; rather, he is using hyperbole to contrast one thing with another.

As we experience what it really means to be a member of God's family, our earthly loves will pale in the blazing light of the heavenly love he will ignite in our hearts. And not incidentally, we'll often grow to disdain the lesser lights that we allow to compete with the true glory that is due God. The closer we grow to our Heavenly Father, the more our hearts will repent as we see how our idolatry wounds him. We'll realize that our misplaced passions are the reason that Christ lays down his life in our place.

It might also be tempting to misinterpret Jesus' statement that whoever does God's will is God's child. Make no mistake; Jesus isn't calling us to legalism. Time and again, he chastises the Pharisees for obeying the Law without understanding his Father's will. Obeying the Law doesn't make us God's children; rather, those who are God's children will seek to obey his Law because they know and love their Father. Not everyone who does godly things is godly, but everyone who knows God will do godly things.

Jesus is revealing a spiritual reality bigger than the Law or tradition. This reality overwhelms disease and demonic oppression. It eclipses the interests of religious and political factions. It's even more profound than the most basic and sacred of all earthly institutions: the family.

In his coming kingdom, the intimacy, trust, and acceptance shared by the children of God will outshine even the deepest relationships of the healthiest of earthly families.

Our biggest ideas of heaven are much too small.

PRAYER: Jesus, remind me that I did not earn a place at your table. Rather, you chose me when I was a disobedient orphan and paid the price for my adoption with your own blood. You chose others and paid their price as well. Therefore, I can be nothing but grateful to you and nothing but loving to the brothers and sisters you have seated around me at your table. Amen.

MARK 4

EPISODE 19

NOT THE SEED, BUT THE SOIL

The parable is a familiar teaching tool for rabbis who know that even the smallest child remembers a story better than a fact. Facts can be flat, disconnected things. But stories have depth, relevance, and the ability to connect with the senses and remain in the memory.

> *4:1 Again Jesus began to teach by the lake. The crowd that gathered around him was so large that he got into a boat and sat in it out on the lake, while all the people were along the shore at the water's edge. 2 He taught them many things by parables, and in his teaching said: 3 "Listen! A farmer went out to sow his seed. 4 As he was scattering the seed, some fell along the path, and the birds came and ate it up. 5 Some fell on rocky places, where it did not have much soil. It sprang up quickly, because the soil was shallow. 6 But when the sun came up, the plants were scorched, and they withered because they had no root.*

7 Other seed fell among thorns, which grew up and choked the plants, so that they did not bear grain. 8 Still other seed fell on good soil. It came up, grew and produced a crop, some multiplying thirty, some sixty, some a hundred times." 9 Then Jesus said, "Whoever has ears to hear, let him hear."

Like Wisdom herself calling out in Solomon's proverbs, Jesus cries, "Hear me!" And he concludes his illustration by implying that listening with the ears and understanding with the heart are two different things.

This particular parable concerns a farmer, some seeds, and different kinds of soil. Simple enough. Yet even his closest followers can't grasp the greater truth hidden in plain sight.

10 When he was alone, the Twelve and the others around him asked him about the parables. 11 He told them, "The secret of the kingdom of God has been given to you. But to those on the outside everything is said in parables 12 so that," 'they may be ever seeing but never perceiving, and ever hearing but never understanding; otherwise they might turn and be forgiven!'"

Jesus' challenge is to teach people about a Father they've never seen, a kingdom they've never visited, and a value system that contradicts everything they've ever known. At the same time, his every word is being scrutinized by religious and political authorities that want to accuse him of blasphemy and treason.

Parables are definitely the way to go.

13 Then Jesus said to them, "Don't you understand this parable? How then will you understand any parable? 14 The farmer sows the word. 15 Some people are like seed along the path, where the word is sown. As soon as they hear it, Satan comes and takes away the word that was sown in them. 16 Others, like seed sown on rocky places, hear the word and at once receive it with joy. 17 But since they have no root, they last only a short time. When trouble or persecution comes because of the word, they quickly fall away. 18 Still others, like seed sown among thorns, hear the word; 19 but the worries of this life, the deceitfulness of wealth and the desires for other things come in and choke the word, making it unfruitful. 20 Others, like seed sown on good soil, hear the word, accept it, and produce a crop—some thirty, some sixty, some a hundred times what was sown."

Every parable answers a central question. So what's the question implied in this story? Perhaps it's, "Why isn't everyone who hears the good news of the Kingdom transformed by it?"

Jesus presents several clear alternatives. Sometimes Satan is the culprit; other times there's a lack of deep commitment. Or the problem may be the trials and temptations of life. But like seed scattered in different places, the truth will inevitably take hold in the lives of some people and grow exponentially— eventually transforming the whole landscape.

While the soil isn't always reliable, the seed is.

PRAYER: Lord, empower me by your grace to prevail when trials and temptations, troubles and persecutions—and even my own fears and selfish desires—become obstacles to obedience. Help me to see that your kingdom is relentlessly expanding and that one day things will be on earth as they are in heaven. In the meantime, help me fix my heart on you, so that my life can be multiplied for your glory. Amen.

EPISODE 20

TO ENGAGE OR DISENGAGE?

Christ follows up the complex parable of the seeds and soils with a short, simple one:

> *4:21 He said to them, "Do you bring in a lamp to put it under a bowl or a bed? Instead, don't you put it on its stand? 22 For whatever is hidden is meant to be disclosed, and whatever is concealed is meant to be brought out into the open. 23 If anyone has ears to hear, let them hear."*

In this case, the parable's central question is: "Should God's people disengage themselves from their culture in order not to be tainted by it?"

Jesus' response is direct and somewhat comedic: no sane person lights an oil lamp just to put it under his or her mattress! The truth's not a secret to be protected but rather a message to be proclaimed.

This particular parable may have been addressed to some contemporary Jewish groups, like the Essenes, who withdrew from the "worldly" culture at large to practice their faith in closed, religious communities.

No, Jesus says, the truth that sets men free must be clearly revealed to the whole world.

There's a difference between the *world* and *worldliness*.

God made the world, sent his Son to redeem the world, and one day will restore the world to all he intends it to be.

On the other hand, *worldliness* is the very spiritual condition from which we need to be delivered. We are worldly when we place ourselves at the center of our universe and demand that all things serve our needs and desires. This self-centeredness eventually snowballs into greed, lust, anger, and idolatry.

God has ordained that those of us who are being delivered from worldliness will become light-bearers to the world. As recipients of his forgiveness, we offer it to others—not with judgmental and condemning attitudes—but rather as those who have become aware of our own spiritual bankruptcy and are experiencing the incomparable riches bestowed upon us by Christ's sacrifice.

We can abandon worldliness, but we can never abandon *the world*—for the world and everything within it are the objects of God's infinite affection.

PRAYER: Lord, deliver me from self-righteous sanctimony: from trying to guard my fragile spirituality by not exposing myself to those who need you most. Help me realize that seeking and saving the lost requires engaging and loving the lost. Likewise, deliver me from my own unrighteousness: I'm often hesitant to proclaim your truth because I'm so deficient in applying it to my own life. I'm afraid that my hypocrisy will be revealed and your Kingdom will be defamed. So give me a bold humility. Help others to see your strength in my weakness and your sufficiency in my inadequacy. And when I use words to proclaim your gospel, let those words be inspired by your Spirit and persuasive to people's hearts and minds. Amen.

EPISODE 21

MEASURED BY HOW
WE MEASURE

Next, Jesus places a pair of proverbs among his parables. A proverb is a simple saying that reveals a profound truth. It's another familiar teaching device used by rabbis.

> *4:24 "Consider carefully what you hear," he continued. "With the measure you use, it will be measured to you—and even more.*

When we buy a pound of coffee beans, we hope the scales are honest and that we're not getting less than what we've paid for. Similarly, it would be unreasonable to expect others to treat us honestly if we shortchange them. But Jesus isn't just talking about beans.

Some in the crowd are there to criticize Christ, not to follow him. Jesus warns his listeners that those who judge others harshly will one day be held to that same, severe standard. Likewise, those who regard others with grace and mercy will receive even more in kind. The door swings both ways.

25 Whoever has will be given more; whoever does not have, even what they have will be taken from them."

Although it may seem unfair for Jesus to say that what little someone has will be taken from him and given to someone who already has more, this result is not a function of the "giver" but rather of the "receiver."

It's been said that our lives are either leaky buckets or overflowing wellsprings. If we are excessively judgmental and critical, then whatever resources we have will eventually leak out of our lives and dissipate. But if we allow Christ's love to flow through us and transform us, then our capacity to bless others will increase—as will God's capacity to bless us.

PRAYER: Lord, help me carefully consider that you will judge my life the way I've judged others. This is a sobering thought because I constantly find myself criticizing my brothers and sisters. So make my life an overflowing wellspring of your grace rather than a leaky bucket from which everything will eventually drain. Even when I'm called to admonish and discipline others, help me do so with the same love and compassion with which you correct me. Amen.

EPISODE 22

TWO MORE SEED ANALOGIES

J esus offers two more parables to describe his
Father's kingdom.

> *4:26 He also said, "This is what the kingdom of God
> is like. A man scatters seed on the ground. 27 Night
> and day, whether he sleeps or gets up, the seed sprouts
> and grows, though he does not know how. 28 All by
> itself the soil produces grain—first the stalk, then the
> head, then the full kernel in the head. 29 As soon as
> the grain is ripe, he puts the sickle to it, because the
> harvest has come."*

The Greek word for "parable" means
"comparison" or "alongside." So when Jesus says, "the
kingdom of God is like..." he's using something
familiar to illustrate something unfamiliar. In this case,
the unknown reality is the kingdom of God, a
dominion no human has yet experienced...and an
unstoppable force that will eventually transform all of
creation.

Jesus returns to the imagery of a farmer planting
seed. After the seed is planted, it grows. The seed has a
relentless life-force of its own, so powerful that the

farmer doesn't even need to understand how it works...it just does, day in and day out. Eventually, the crop matures, and the farmer harvests it.

Likewise, God's kingdom is unstoppable and inevitable. Though it begins as little seeds, it will produce a huge harvest in due time. Jesus then tells a similar parable to underscore the truth he has just revealed:

> *30 Again he said, "What shall we say the kingdom of God is like, or what parable shall we use to describe it? 31 It is like a mustard seed, which is the smallest of all seeds on earth. 32 Yet when planted, it grows and becomes the largest of all garden plants, with such big branches that the birds can perch in its shade."*

Mustard seeds are not literally the smallest seeds and mustard trees are not really the largest trees. But Jesus is not making a scientific observation. Rather, he's using hyperbole to show how something seemingly insignificant can grow into something absolutely enormous.

It's as if he's saying, *"I know it doesn't look like much now. But just show a little faith. Give it a little time. One day, my kingdom will offer safety and sanctuary to the whole world."*

PRAYER: Heavenly Father, your Kingdom is relentless—replacing death with life and darkness with light. I don't have to fear or be anxious about its success—for Christ guaranteed that on the cross. Rather, all I have to be is faithful. Your kingdom will come. Your will be done on earth as it is in heaven. So let your kingdom grow in me today. Amen.

EPISODE 23

A TERRIFYING STORM

4:33 With many similar parables Jesus spoke the word to them, as much as they could understand. 34 He did not say anything to them without using a parable. But when he was alone with his own disciples, he explained everything.

Jesus is God. Not just *godly*, but *God*. God, the Utterly Other.

No wonder the Twelve follow him and the crowds swarm him. Jesus reveals as much as they can understand—and more. He uses word pictures because words alone are not enough. He uses parables to keep those who resist the light in the dark. And when he is alone with his closest followers, he unpacks the truth about his kingdom—and himself—in small enough pieces that they're not annihilated by his revelation.

But every so often, they get totally freaked out.

35 That day when evening came, he said to his disciples, "Let us go over to the other side." 36 Leaving the crowd behind, they took him along, just as he was, in the boat. There were also other boats with him. 37 A furious squall came up, and the waves broke over the boat, so that it was nearly swamped. 38 Jesus was in the stern, sleeping on a cushion. The disciples woke him and said to him, "Teacher, don't you care if we drown?" 39 He got up, rebuked the wind and said to the waves, "Quiet! Be still!" Then the wind died down and it was completely calm. 40 He said to his disciples, "Why are you so afraid? Do you still have no faith?" 41 They were terrified and asked each other, "Who is this? Even the wind and the waves obey him!"

To be honest, I have very little idea how this fully God/fully human thing works. I guess that's why they call it a mystery, a paradox. Jesus, the Son of the inexhaustible God, is exhausted. He's been standing in a small boat, first teaching the multitudes in parables, and then explaining their meanings to the Twelve. That evening, they push away from the shore toward the southeastern coastal area called the Decapolis. Jesus collapses onto a cushion in a dead sleep as a ferocious storm begins to sweep over their little flotilla.

The disciples are terrified. They wake Jesus. He tells the storm to be quiet. The wind and the waves instantly obey.

Now, the disciples are even more terrified. And they are only beginning to catch a glimpse of all that he is.

PRAYER: Jesus, so often the storms of life overwhelm me and I feel like I'm drowning. To make matters worse, sometimes it seems like you're oblivious to my circumstances. Help me to understand that darkness and light, chaos and peace, even heaven and hell are all the same to you. You are their Lord, and what you say goes. Jesus, I pray that you would calm the storm around me—and if that's not your will—that you'd calm the storm in me. Reveal yourself, not only as Master of the Wind and Waves, but also as Lord of my Life. Amen.

MARK 5

EPISODE 24

A LEGION OF DEMONS

5:1 They went across the lake to the region of the Gerasenes. 2 When Jesus got out of the boat, a man with an impure spirit came from the tombs to meet him.

The disciples endure a terrifying night on the Sea of Galilee only to make landfall near—of all places—a cemetery. As soon as they step ashore, a wild-looking man emerges from among the burial vaults and heads straight for Jesus.

3 This man lived in the tombs, and no one could bind him any more, not even with a chain. 4 For he had often been chained hand and foot, but he tore the chains apart and broke the irons on his feet. No one was strong enough to subdue him. 5 Night and day among the tombs and in the hills he would cry out and cut himself with stones.

Mark describes this man as having been "demonized." Attempts to restrain him fail because the power within him exercises supernatural strength. These spirits torture him to the brink of death but leave him alive so that they might continue their torment.

> *6 When he saw Jesus from a distance, he ran and fell on his knees in front of him. 7 He shouted at the top of his voice, "What do you want with me, Jesus, Son of the Most High God? In God's name don't torture me!"*

Imagine the irony: the spirits that have been torturing this man are now begging to be spared from torture! They even plead that God's Son swear by his own Father to grant them this mercy.

> *8 For Jesus had said to him, "Come out of this man, you impure spirit!" 9 Then Jesus asked him, "What is your name?" "My name is Legion," he replied, "for we are many."*

The Messiah's mission is to free captives from their bondage. Whether by choice or chance, this pitiful man's life had become a breeding ground for demonic activity. When Jesus asks his name, he responds that "he" is actually a "we," a veritable legion of spirits. As a point of reference, a Roman military legion was comprised of 6000 infantry and 120 armed horsemen; so calling himself "Legion" indicates the considerable satanic power and presence now bowing before Christ.

10 And he begged Jesus again and again not to send them out of the area. 11 A large herd of pigs was feeding on the nearby hillside. 12 The demons begged Jesus, "Send us among the pigs; allow us to go into them."

One of the strangest stories in the New Testament now gets even stranger:

13 He gave them permission, and the evil spirits came out and went into the pigs. The herd, about two thousand in number, rushed down the steep bank into the lake and were drowned.

It may be that Jesus allows these spirits to retreat from their human host into a herd of swine so that he can efficiently dispatch them from this world altogether. Fully within his rights as Creator and Messiah, Jesus sacrifices these animals to deliver this man and this region from the deadly power of these demonic spirits.

This miracle does not go unnoticed by the community. But where heaven sees the destruction of a legion of demonic forces, the locals just see drowned pigs. To those without spiritual vision, it's not a pretty sight.

14 Those tending the pigs ran off and reported this in the town and countryside, and the people went out to see what had happened. 15 When they came to Jesus, they saw the man who had been possessed by the legion of demons, sitting there, dressed and in his right mind; and they were afraid. 16 Those who had seen it told the people what had happened to the demon-possessed man—and told about the pigs as well. 17 Then the people began to plead with Jesus to leave their region.

There is probably no individual in all of Scripture whose life seems more hopeless than this "Man of the Tombs." And yet, here he sits—dressed and in his sound mind—silently testifying that there is no physical, mental or spiritual condition that God's love and mercy can't transform.

While the townspeople are understandably upset about the death of their pigs, they seem to be even more frightened that this demon-possessed maniac is now sitting, sane and civil, at the feet of Christ. This is just too much for them.

The inhabitants of the ten cities of the Decapolis are principally Greek. Some scholars believe they may have been actively worshiping these demons, believing them to be the ancient spirits of those who lived during Greece's Golden Age. So while many communities are rushing out to meet Jesus, this town is literally begging him to leave.

He does.

18 As Jesus was getting into the boat, the man who had been demon-possessed begged to go with him. 19 Jesus did not let him, but said, "Go home to your family and tell them how much the Lord has done for you, and how he has had mercy on you." 20 So the man went away and began to tell in the Decapolis how much Jesus had done for him. And all the people were amazed.

On this occasion, rather than telling the man to keep silent about the miracle, Christ commands him to tell his Greek friends and neighbors about God's mercy. And he obeys.

PRAYER: Jesus, you have authority over every spiritual power in the universe—whether evil or good. Free me from whatever enslaves me that isn't you. Deliver me from anything destructive that possesses my mind or oppresses my spirit. Help me understand that the spiritual war raging around me has already been won at the cross. Help me believe that those whose lives have been devastated by sickness and sin can find true healing and wholeness in you. Let me imagine them as you do: whole and healthy at your feet. For you are our deliverer. Amen.

EPISODE 25

JAIRUS' LAST RESORT

What happens next is a miracle within a miracle.

5:21 When Jesus had again crossed over by boat to the other side of the lake, a large crowd gathered around him while he was by the lake. 22 Then one of the synagogue rulers, named Jairus, came, and when he saw Jesus, he fell at his feet. 23 He pleaded earnestly with him, "My little daughter is dying. Please come and put your hands on her so that she will be healed and live."

Jairus is a synagogue leader and, by definition, probably not one of Jesus' biggest fans. The last thing the religious bureaucracy needs is a Jewish zealot claiming to be the Messiah, stirring up the people's hopes of deliverance from their Roman occupiers.

About forty years hence, in 70 AD, Titus and his Roman legions will sweep into Jerusalem to quell the swelling political unrest. They'll slaughter its inhabitants and destroy the beautiful Temple that Herod the Great had built to ingratiate himself with the Jews. Historians record that the devastation is so complete that not one stone is left standing upon another.

But beyond their political issues with Jesus, Jairus' colleagues are offended that this carpenter from Nazareth would call himself God's Son. This is blasphemy, punishable by death under the Jewish law. Because of the Roman occupation, the Jewish officials lack the authority to put a man to death without the Roman governor's approval. This is why the religious leaders will arrange a sunrise trial with Pontius Pilate to have Jesus crucified by the Romans.

The majority of synagogue leaders are fiercely opposed to Jesus on both political and spiritual grounds. They are also jealous of Jesus' tremendous popularity among their people. And yet Mark records that Jairus, a respected spiritual and civil leader, somehow elbows his way through the teeming crowd to fall at Jesus' feet and beg him to come to his home.

Why?

Because his 12-year-old daughter is dying.

And Jesus is his last resort.

Jairus has probably hired the best physicians in the region. No improvement. He has solicited the prayers of the most spiritual priests in the nation. No change.

Jairus has tried everything, and now, he tries Jesus. Jesus: the outlaw, the blasphemer, the Sabbath-breaker. Jesus: who consorts with tax-collectors, Samaritan half-breeds, and prostitutes. Jesus: the one who has just calmed a raging storm and delivered a demon-possessed man from a lifetime of torment.

Jesus: his last resort.

Jairus begs Jesus to come—and miraculously—he agrees. But the burgeoning crowd that meets Jesus at the lakeshore comes as well. A moving mob of humanity. *"Coming to my home,"* Jairus probably thinks, *"Who cares if they will make my house unclean...at least Jesus will be there!"*

PRAYER: Jesus, why is it I only turn to you after I exhaust every other option? I turn to science, logic, and learning before I turn to you. I turn to money, power, and position before I turn to you. It seems that you are my last resort instead of my first response. Lord of Creation, create in me a heart that immediately casts every care upon you. For no one loves me—or those I love—more than you. Help me trust you in the midst of impossible circumstances, understanding that you will either deliver me from them...or deliver me through them. Amen.

EPISODE 26

A SICK WOMAN'S LAST RESORT

5:24 So Jesus went with him. A large crowd followed and pressed around him. 25 And a woman was there who had been subject to bleeding for twelve years.

For twelve agonizing years she has been bleeding. Her condition has made her ceremonially unclean. She is shunned by her community and barred from her synagogue.

Where's her husband? She either doesn't have one, or he's too ashamed to be seen with her.

26 She had suffered a great deal under the care of many doctors and had spent all she had, yet instead of getting better she grew worse.

She, like Jairus, has tried everything. Gathering up what few mites of money she has left, the physicians are called. No improvement. She prays night after night, weeping in her private prison. No change.

Sometimes she wonders which is worse: the sickness of her body or the death of her spirit?

27 When she heard about Jesus, she came up behind him in the crowd and touched his cloak, 28 because she thought, "If I just touch his clothes, I will be healed."

She hears there's a prophet from Galilee whose teachings are being validated by divine miracles. She's tried everything; now she will try Jesus, her last resort. And with what little faith she can summon up through a dozen years of suffering, she slips through the crowd and reaches out to touch the hem of his robe.

29 Immediately her bleeding stopped and she felt in her body that she was freed from her suffering. 30 At once Jesus realized that power had gone out from him. He turned around in the crowd and asked, "Who touched my clothes?"

The crowd almost crushes Jesus as it surges forward. People are pressed shoulder to shoulder, and some are lifted off their feet. Many struggle against being trampled down. But then Jesus stops. *"Someone has touched me,"* he says.

31 "You see the people crowding against you," his disciples answered, "and yet you can ask, 'Who touched me?' " 32 But Jesus kept looking around to see who had done it.

His disciples tell him that it's impossible to tell who has touched him. If I were Jairus, I would be panicking, *"We have no time for this woman...my daughter is dying. We must go! Now!"*

33 Then the woman, knowing what had happened to her, came and fell at his feet and, trembling with fear, told him the whole truth.

The woman who's been suffering for the past twelve years—ironically, for the same number of years that Jairus' daughter has lived—speaks up. *"I thought...I know a holy man would never touch me to heal me...and I could never defile the Rabbi by touching him...so I thought if only I could touch the hem of your robe I would be healed. And immediately, the bleeding stopped and I was made whole."*

34 He said to her, "Daughter, your faith has healed you. Go in peace and be freed from your suffering."

PRAYER: Lord, turn my despair into desperation. Rather than surrendering to my pain and hopelessness, give me the audacity to push through the crowd to touch you. For out of such desperation comes real faith, and from such faith comes healing and transformation. Amen.

EPISODE 27

WHEN OUR WORST NIGHTMARE COMES TRUE

A s this unnamed woman's twelve-year ordeal ends, so does the life of Jairus' 12-year old daughter.

> *5:35 While Jesus was still speaking, some men came from the house of Jairus, the synagogue ruler. "Your daughter is dead," they said. "Why bother the teacher any more?" 36 Overhearing what they said, Jesus told him, "Don't be afraid; just believe."*

How could Jairus not be crushed? His worst fears have just come true. And to add insult to injury, an unclean woman has interrupted Jesus on his way to heal his daughter and "hijacked" the very miracle for which Jairus and his wife have prayed and sacrificed and begged. And yet, Jesus responds with the most common words spoken by heaven to humanity throughout Scripture: "Don't be afraid."

> *37 He did not let anyone follow him except Peter, James and John the brother of James.*

Somehow, Jesus escapes the crowd and the rest of the Twelve and proceeds with his inner circle of disciples.

38 When they came to the home of the synagogue ruler, Jesus saw a commotion, with people crying and wailing loudly.

As they approach Jairus' home, they begin to hear the sounds of those who are gathering to weep with his family. In a culture where the infant mortality rate is 30% and most people don't live past 40, "professional mourners" make their living by singing, playing instruments, and grieving loudly to demonstrate affection for the dead. The bigger the crowd, the more beloved the departed one. It's akin to our modern custom of buying the most expensive casket to show how much we loved the one who died.

39 He went in and said to them, "Why all this commotion and wailing? The child is not dead but asleep." 40 But they laughed at him. After he put them all out, he took the child's father and mother and the disciples who were with him, and went in where the child was. 41 He took her by the hand and said to her, "Talitha koum!" (which means, "Little girl, I say to you, get up!").

Jesus sends the mourners and mockers away and then enters the room where the little girl's body lay. Her corpse is motionless. She is truly dead. But just as Jesus' simple words calmed the deadly storm, he takes her hand and says, *"My child, get up"* and Death—itself a consequence of the Fall—obeys.

42 Immediately the girl stood up and walked around (she was twelve years old). At this they were completely astonished.

Coagulated blood becomes liquefied and flows. Lifeless lungs begin to convert air into usable oxygen in the bloodstream. Dead brain cells regenerate, and rigor mortis is reversed.

The same One who created life from the dust of the ground in Eden has again animated the inanimate, demonstrating that he is not only the Way and the Truth—but Life himself. Christ can raise the dead with just his word, for he is life.

43 He gave strict orders not to let anyone know about this, and told them to give her something to eat.

To prove that their little girl was alive and not merely a ghost, Jesus tells Jairus and his wife to give her something to eat. He then warns them to keep this matter to themselves. In contrast to the Decapolis, the crowds in this region are already overwhelming and perhaps even hampering Jesus' efforts to travel from village to village.

But who can keep so big a secret to themselves?

PRAYER: Jesus, sometimes our worst nightmares come true: sickness, suffering, death, betrayal, and loss. And yet, we hear your compassionate voice whispering, "Don't be afraid. Things are not as they seem." And they aren't. For you turn mourning into dancing, weeping into singing, and trials into character. You even undo Death—if not temporarily in this life—then ultimately for time and eternity. There is nothing that can separate us from your love. Every overwhelming circumstance becomes another opportunity for us to trust you more deeply— and therefore experience your love more profoundly. Help me trust you in the dark of night, knowing that the dawn is closer now than ever. Amen.

MARK 6

EPISODE 28

A PROPHET WITHOUT HONOR

Years ago, I traveled to New York City on business. I was walking the streets of Manhattan but couldn't seem to find The Empire State Building. Completed in 1931, it's still one of the tallest and most majestic buildings in the world. I stopped someone to ask where it was, and he laughed and said, "You're right beside it. When you're this close, it's easy to miss."

Sure enough, I was standing in its shadow. There at its base, it looked like all the other skyscrapers around me. I had to get some distance from it to truly appreciate its breathtaking grandeur. Likewise, those closest to Jesus had a similar problem seeing the true nature of the man standing in their presence.

6:1 Jesus left there and went to his hometown, accompanied by his disciples. 2 When the Sabbath came, he began to teach in the synagogue, and many who heard him were amazed. "Where did this man get these things?" they asked. "What's this wisdom that has been given him? What are these remarkable miracles he is performing? 3 Isn't this the carpenter? Isn't this Mary's son and the brother of James, Joseph, Judas and Simon? Aren't his sisters here with us?" And they took offense at him. 4 Jesus said to them, "A prophet is not without honor except in his own town, among his relatives and in his own home."

Sadly, Jesus' neighbors and kinsfolk fail to recognize the Son of God in their midst. While they're astonished by his wisdom and miracles, they still doubt his divinity. After all, they reason, Jesus grew up here with his brothers and sisters. How could something so extraordinary come from someone who seems so ordinary? Their rational perspective blinds them to the greater truth.

5 He could not do any miracles there, except lay his hands on a few sick people and heal them. 6a And he was amazed at their lack of faith.

While faith bears fruit, doubt does not. Because God rewards those who eagerly seek him, we shouldn't be surprised when the Lord withholds blessing from those who actively doubt his character.

How ironic! Time after time, crowds throughout Israel are amazed at Jesus' authority, teaching, and miracles. And yet, in Jesus' hometown, Mark records that Christ himself is amazed by *their* lack of faith.

PRAYER: Jesus, I don't want you to be amazed by my lack of faith. Help me not only understand your goodness, but also your God-ness. Help me not only confess you as God's Son, but also trust you as my Savior. Let me not only accept your words, but your authority in my life as well. I pray that you would be honored by my faith in you rather than amazed by my doubt. Amen.

EPISODE 29

POURED IN TO BE POURED OUT

6:6b Then Jesus went around teaching from village to village. 7 Calling the Twelve to him, he began to send them out two by two and gave them authority over impure spirits. 8 These were his instructions: "Take nothing for the journey except a staff—no bread, no bag, no money in your belts. 9 Wear sandals but not an extra shirt. 10 Whenever you enter a house, stay there until you leave that town. 11 And if any place will not welcome you or listen to you, leave that place and shake the dust off your feet as a testimony against them."

The Twelve see Jesus preach, heal, and deliver. Now, it's their turn. Jesus pairs them up and sends them out. He gives them his divine authority and simple instructions on how to conduct themselves.

These are training missions.

By commanding that they take only the basics with them, he's teaching them to live by faith and not my sight. By telling them to stay in one home and not move when a better offer comes along, he's teaching them to prioritize their mission above their personal comfort. By acknowledging that some people will be adversarial to their message, he's teaching them that it's better to be faithful than popular.

12 They went out and preached that people should repent. 13 They drove out many demons and anointed many sick people with oil and healed them.

Jesus pours himself into these men so that they might pour themselves into others. The Twelve become authentic imitators of Jesus. The gospel is preached, lives are transformed, spiritual shackles are broken, and the sick are healed. The kingdom's tiny mustard seed is now growing and spreading its branches across Israel. For those who have eyes to see and ears to hear, the Messianic prophecies are being fulfilled in their presence.

PRAYER: Lord, pour yourself into me so that I might pour myself into others. Help me go in your authority, preach in your name, and heal by your power. Duplicate yourself in me, and multiply your kingdom through me. Amen.

VINCE WILCOX

EPISODE 30

JOHN THE BAPTIZER BEHEADED

The Jews are not the only ones who notice what Jesus and his followers are doing:

> *6:14 King Herod heard about this, for Jesus' name had become well known. Some were saying, "John the Baptist has been raised from the dead, and that is why miraculous powers are at work in him." 15 Others said, "He is Elijah." And still others claimed, "He is a prophet, like one of the prophets of long ago." 16 But when Herod heard this, he said, "John, the man I beheaded, has been raised from the dead!"*

Herod Antipas is the son of Herod the Great, the Roman king who rules Galilee at the birth of Christ. You may be familiar with the story of Herod and the magi, "wise men" from the East who follow a star in search of the newborn "King of the Jews." Herod the Great commands the magi to report back to him when they have found this infant so that he might supposedly go and worship him as well. The wise men disobey and return to their homeland a different way after finding Mary, Joseph, and the baby Jesus. Undeterred in his paranoia, Herod then orders the slaughter of all the young male children in the area.

After Herod's own death, governance of his region is divided among his three sons, who are now technically "tetrarchs" rather than kings. Herod Antipas the Tetrarch seems to be no less self-indulgent than his father. He divorces his own wife to marry his brother's wife, Herodias. Although this probably isn't that scandalous to the Romans, these actions are unconscionable to the Jews. And since Herod and Herodias rule the Jews, having a rogue Jewish prophet heaping criticism on them doesn't sit well.

17 For Herod himself had given orders to have John arrested, and he had him bound and put in prison. He did this because of Herodias, his brother Philip's wife, whom he had married. 18 For John had been saying to Herod, "It is not lawful for you to have your brother's wife." 19 So Herodias nursed a grudge against John and wanted to kill him. But she was not able to, 20 because Herod feared John and protected him, knowing him to be a righteous and holy man. When Herod heard John, he was greatly puzzled; yet he liked to listen to him.

John's condemnation infuriates Herodias and she looks for a way to silence him permanently.

21 Finally the opportune time came. On his birthday Herod gave a banquet for his high officials and military commanders and the leading men of Galilee. 22 When the daughter of Herodias came in and danced, she pleased Herod and his dinner guests. The king said to the girl, "Ask me for anything you want, and I'll give it to you." 23 And he promised her with an oath, "Whatever you ask I will give you, up to half my kingdom." 24 She went out and said to her mother, "What shall I ask for?" "The head of John the Baptist," she answered. 25 At once the girl hurried in to the king with the request: "I want you to give me right now the head of John the Baptist on a platter." 26 The king was greatly distressed, but because of his oaths and his dinner guests, he did not want to refuse her. 27 So he immediately sent an executioner with orders to bring John's head. The man went, beheaded John in the prison, 28 and brought back his head on a platter. He presented it to the girl, and she gave it to her mother. 29 On hearing of this, John's disciples came and took his body and laid it in a tomb.

By any standard, this is a lurid affair. A politically ambitious queen presses her egotistical husband to falsely imprison a troublesome preacher. Fueled by drunken lust, the ruler makes a reckless public promise to his sexy stepdaughter that ends in the decapitation and symbolic dishonoring of a popular prophet.

PRAYER: Father in Heaven, not much has changed in two thousand years. The love of money, sex, and power continues to wage war on our souls. Politicians continue to curry favor with their constituents. The rich and famous boldly flaunt their immorality. Drunken lust results in regrettable acts. And godliness takes a beating. Lord, help me to realize three things. First: without your transforming power in my life, "there but for the grace of God go I." Second: although it seems that darkness prevails, your coming kingdom is nearer now than ever. And finally: those who are persecuted for your Name's sake will be exalted in your presence. Until that day, help me live a life of godly expectation. Amen.

EPISODE 31

AN INVITATION TO REST

Jesus knows that the spiritual welfare of his disciples is connected to their physical well-being, so he pulls them aside to eat and rest.

> *6:30 The apostles gathered around Jesus and reported to him all they had done and taught. 31 Then, because so many people were coming and going that they did not even have a chance to eat, he said to them, "Come with me by yourselves to a quiet place and get some rest." 32 So they went away by themselves in a boat to a solitary place.*

Earlier in Mark's Gospel, Jesus tells the disciples that he is Lord of the Sabbath (2:28). In this passage, we see that he's not only Lord of the day of rest, but he's actually the rest his followers' souls and bodies need. For true rest is not just the absence of activity, but rather his active presence in our midst.

From the biblical account of Creation to the giving of the Law at Sinai, we see that rest properly follows work. We shouldn't fool ourselves into thinking that other people's needs are always more important than our own.

Unless we allow ourselves proper time for rest and refreshment, we'll be of little use to the Lord and those he's called us to serve. To paraphrase St. Augustine, God created us to need rest so that we might find our rest in him.

PRAYER: Lord, thank you for caring deeply about my physical and spiritual health. Help me develop the habit of getting alone with you, pouring out my life to you, and having my soul fed and refreshed by you. Amen.

EPISODE 32

"YOU GIVE THEM SOMETHING TO EAT"

6:33 But many who saw them leaving recognized them and ran on foot from all the towns and got there ahead of them. 34 When Jesus landed and saw a large crowd, he had compassion on them, because they were like sheep without a shepherd. So he began teaching them many things.

By now, Jesus is so popular that large crowds flock to wherever he's headed. When he arrives, the multitude spreads as far as the eye can see, their light-colored robes reflecting the heat of the Middle East sun like thousands of sheep dotting the landscape. His heart goes out to his lambs and the Good Shepherd begins to reveal his Father's kingdom to them.

35 By this time it was late in the day, so his disciples came to him. "This is a remote place," they said, "and it's already very late. 36 Send the people away so they can go to the surrounding countryside and villages and buy themselves something to eat." 37 But he answered,

"You give them something to eat." They said to him, "That would take eight months of a man's wages! Are we to go and spend that much on bread and give it to them to eat?"

This is a teachable moment for the disciples: not just about Jesus' sufficiency but about their responsibility. He truly expects his disciples to serve those they lead. He requires them to put others' needs before their own. Today, over one billion people go to bed hungry. Christ's command for us to feed his sheep is more relevant than ever.

38 "How many loaves do you have?" he asked. "Go and see." When they found out, they said, "Five— and two fish."

Our inadequacy becomes the opportunity for God's provision. Our hunger becomes the occasion for his glory. Jesus' character and power is revealed is his miraculous meeting of a basic human need. And his disciples are privileged to be an integral part of that miracle.

39 Then Jesus directed them to have all the people sit down in groups on the green grass. 40 So they sat down in groups of hundreds and fifties. 41 Taking the five loaves and the two fish and looking up to heaven, he gave thanks and broke the loaves. Then he gave them to his disciples to distribute to the people. He also divided the two fish among them all. 42 They all ate and were satisfied, 43 and the disciples picked up twelve basketfuls of broken pieces of bread and fish.

44 The number of the men who had eaten was five thousand.

This number does not include the women and children among them. Christ not only demonstrates his lordship over death, demons, and disease; he also reveals his ability to meet the basic needs of everyday life. This provision would have reminded every Jew of God's miraculous feeding of the nation of Israel in the desert by means of manna sent from heaven. But this time, the disciples become the means by which the multitude is fed.

PRAYER: Jesus, give me a heart for the hungry. Let me not be overwhelmed by the magnitude of the need but rather by the privilege of sharing what I have with those your Father loves. I pray that you will multiply my meager gifts to meet the needs of the multitude. Then we will all eat and be satisfied. In your name I pray. Amen.

EPISODE 33

WALKING ON WATER

6:45 Immediately Jesus made his disciples get into the boat and go on ahead of him to Bethsaida, while he dismissed the crowd.

The undeniable evidence for Jesus' Messiah-ship continues to mount. By sending his disciples ahead of him, Jesus sets in motion another event where his supernatural nature will be revealed.

46 After leaving them, he went up on a mountainside to pray. 47 Later that night, the boat was in the middle of the lake, and he was alone on land. 48 He saw the disciples straining at the oars, because the wind was against them. Shortly before dawn he went out to them, walking on the lake. He was about to pass by them, 49 but when they saw him walking on the lake, they thought he was a ghost. They cried out, 50 because they all saw him and were terrified. Immediately he spoke to them and said, "Take courage! It is I. Don't be afraid." 51 Then he climbed into the boat with them, and the wind died down. They were completely amazed, 52 for they had not understood about the loaves; their hearts were hardened.

The Twelve are ordinary men who follow an unconventional rabbi from Galilee. Jesus understands that their faith is weak and their hearts are rigid from generations of legalism and oppression. Even though they walk with Jesus every day, they're often blind to the bigger story. So Jesus rocks their world by healing on the Sabbath, touching the untouchable, casting demons into pigs, feeding hungry thousands, and walking on water in the dead of night.

Sometimes the disciples get it; other times they don't. They are alternately terrified, amazed, confused, and elated. I can sympathize with them. This Messiah is stranger than fiction, wilder than our imaginations, and yet filled with profound compassion for the brokenhearted, hurting, and oppressed.

53 When they had crossed over, they landed at Gennesaret and anchored there. 54 As soon as they got out of the boat, people recognized Jesus. 55 They ran throughout that whole region and carried the sick on mats to wherever they heard he was. 56 And wherever he went—into villages, towns or countryside—they placed the sick in the marketplaces. They begged him to let them touch even the edge of his cloak, and all who touched him were healed.

Jesus uses the swift passage across the Sea of Galilee as a means to spread his message throughout the region. He and his men now land their boat at Gennesaret on the northwestern shore of the large lake. As usual, he is greeted by a teeming crowd, seeking to be taught, touched, and healed.

PRAYER: Lord, I must confess that I'm confused—and maybe even a little terrified—when I catch a glimpse of who you really are. Turn my confusion into confidence and my fear into amazement. Help me not only get "it" but get "you." Thrill my soul. Soften my heart. Renew my mind so that I may begin to expect the unexpected. Amen.

MARK 7

EPISODE 34

TURNING LAW INTO LEGALISM

7:1 The Pharisees and some of the teachers of the law who had come from Jerusalem gathered around Jesus 2 and saw some of his disciples eating food with hands that were defiled, that is, unwashed. 3 (The Pharisees and all the Jews do not eat unless they give their hands a ceremonial washing, holding to the tradition of the elders. 4 When they come from the marketplace they do not eat unless they wash. And they observe many other traditions, such as the washing of cups, pitchers and kettles.) 5 So the Pharisees and teachers of the law asked Jesus, "Why don't your disciples live according to the tradition of the elders instead of eating their food with defiled hands?"

Jesus' fame troubles Israel's religious leaders, who send an "inspection team" from Jerusalem to check him out. One of the first things they notice is that some of his followers don't observe the elaborate hand-washing rituals that "true" Jews practice before their meals. Mark comments that these habits are in addition to scores of other customs.

So where did these rules come from?

Some of them were given to Moses by God and meant for all of God's people. Some were given especially for the priests and Levites—since their lives were to be particularly set apart. Still other rules were man-made traditions that developed over the generations.

God's Law reflects who he is and what he values. His character is both loving and just, so he insists that his children live lives of compassion and integrity. Our Heavenly Father values his reputation—his own glory—as well as the welfare of his children.

Scripture testifies that God gave us the Law so that we might live rightly with him and with one another. Like a loving parent, he provides specific structure, discipline, and correction so that we can become what he intends for us to be. Some rules—like dietary restrictions—had tremendous health benefits, a fact that has been confirmed by modern scientists and dieticians. Other rules, like observing the Sabbath and circumcision, were covenantal signs that differentiated the Jews from the pagan nations that surrounded them. But the Law had an even deeper function: to reveal humanity's sinfulness and God's provision for that sin.

The Lord gave the Jews these regulations for his glory and their good. But too often they took the commands of a loving, heavenly Father and turned them into conditions for his love. They couldn't comprehend that godly obedience was to be the result of our relationship with God, not its prerequisite.

God's people took God's constructive rules for living, mixed in their own self-righteous traditions, and ended up with an impossibly frustrating religion that did not glorify God or benefit his children.

PRAYER: Lord, help me learn to love your Law because it's a reflection of your character and values. Help me hunger for your Word and thirst for your righteousness. Free me from legalism and any sense of self-justification. Jesus, you fulfilled every requirement of the Law on my behalf. So my obedience is to please you, not appease you. Let my character bear witness to yours so that those who don't know you will want to. Amen.

EPISODE 35

BECOMING TRULY KOSHER

7:6 He replied, "Isaiah was right when he prophesied about you hypocrites; as it is written: 'These people honor me with their lips, but their hearts are far from me. 7 They worship me in vain; their teachings are merely human rules.' 8 You have let go of the commands of God and are holding on to human traditions." 9 And he continued: "You have a fine way of setting aside the commands of God in order to observe your own traditions! 10 For Moses said, 'Honor your father and your mother,' and, 'Anyone who curses his father or mother must be put to death.' 11 But you say that if anyone declares that what might have been used to help their father or mother is Corban (that is, devoted to God)—12 then you no longer let them do anything for their father or mother. 13 Thus you nullify the word of God by your tradition that you have handed down. And you do many things like that."

Jesus is angry. Very angry.
God's people had contorted his Law to serve selfish ends. Specifically, Christ attacks a rabbinical loophole

that allowed people to designate part of their financial assets as "Corban" (which literally means "temple gift"). By doing this, they could retain constructive possession of their property without having to spend those resources on things like caring for their aging parents. Jesus harshly condemns those who teach that the letter of a man-made law can be used to escape responsibility for a God-given obligation.

But Christ's point isn't just to expose the Pharisee's hypocrisy; rather, he wants us to recognize the sinfulness at work in our own lives.

> *14 Again Jesus called the crowd to him and said, "Listen to me, everyone, and understand this. 15 Nothing outside a person can defile them by going into them. Rather, it is what comes out of a person that defiles them 16 [If anyone has ears to hear, let them hear."] 17 After he had left the crowd and entered the house, his disciples asked him about this parable. 18 "Are you so dull?" he asked. "Don't you see that nothing that enters a person from the outside can defile them? 19 For it doesn't go into their heart but into their stomach, and then out of the body." (In saying this, Jesus declared all foods "clean.") 20 He went on: "What comes out of a person is what defiles them. 21 For it is from within, out of a person's heart, that evil thoughts come--sexual immorality, theft, murder, adultery, 22 greed, malice, deceit, lewdness, envy, slander, arrogance and folly. 23 All these evils come from inside and defile a person."*

Jesus stands in direct opposition to the conventional wisdom of his age. While the Jews teach that eating "kosher" food helps make them pure before God, Christ proclaims that the focal point for sin is the spiritual heart, not the literal stomach. The evil within a man can't be cured by what he eats. Rather, God commands an inner obedience that can't be achieved through an external checklist no matter how comprehensive.

It starts with the heart.

PRAYER: Lord, deliver me from the kind of self-righteousness that uses the Law or tradition to validate my own self-centeredness. Shine your light upon the dark places of my heart. Reveal my sin. Help me be honest with myself and repentant before you. Make me truly "kosher"—pure from the inside out. In your name and by the power of your Spirit I pray. Amen.

EPISODE 36

AN AUDACIOUS FAITH

7:24 Jesus left that place and went to the vicinity of Tyre. He entered a house and did not want anyone to know it; yet he could not keep his presence secret.

It appears that Jesus and his disciples have yet to achieve a measure of rest from the teeming crowds. So they journey north out of Israel toward the Mediterranean port city of Tyre in the region of Syrian Phoenicia. But just as he seems to find some peace and quiet, his rest is interrupted.

> *25 In fact, as soon as she heard about him, a woman whose little daughter was possessed by an impure spirit came and fell at his feet. 26 The woman was a Greek, born in Syrian Phoenicia. She begged Jesus to drive the demon out of her daughter.*

No matter the circumstance, Jesus never ignores the pleas of those on their knees. It's ironic that Jesus encounters a non-Jew begging for his intervention so soon after facing such pushback from the Jewish leaders.

27 "First let the children eat all they want," he told her, "for it is not right to take the children's bread and toss it to the dogs."

Please don't take offense.

Jesus is not implying that this woman is a dog. Rather, he's using a figure of speech—this time a metaphor—to communicate a deeper truth. The original Greek indicates that the word for "dog" used here means a familiar household pet. Perhaps he's saying something like, *"Just as it would be inappropriate to give your pets the family's food before they have had a chance to eat it, the non-Jewish world will have to wait until the Jewish world has had their chance at the table of God's grace."*

Undaunted by his response, this determined woman smartly co-ops Jesus' own metaphor to make her case:

28 "Lord," she replied, "even the dogs under the table eat the children's crumbs." 29 Then he told her, "For such a reply, you may go; the demon has left your daughter." 30 She went home and found her child lying on the bed, and the demon gone.

Her reply pleases Jesus. In her heart, she knows that the Jewish Messiah has come for her as well. For God has been facilitating the redemption of the whole world through the nation of Israel. After the resurrection and Pentecost, the Gospel will literally explode throughout the non-Jewish world. This audacious woman and her daughter simply get a head start.

PRAYER: Lord, help me learn to be audacious when it comes to asking you for difficult things. Let me be relentless in interceding for those I love. Help me understand that you reward those who diligently seek you. Amen.

EPISODE 37

A DEAF MAN HEARS AND SPEAKS

7:31 Then Jesus left the vicinity of Tyre and went through Sidon, down to the Sea of Galilee and into the region of the Decapolis. 32 There some people brought to him a man who was deaf and could hardly talk, and they begged Jesus to place his hand on the man. 33 After he took him aside, away from the crowd, Jesus put his fingers into the man's ears. Then he spit and touched the man's tongue. 34 He looked up to heaven and with a deep sigh said to him, "Ephphatha!" (which means, "Be opened!"). 35 At this, the man's ears were opened, his tongue was loosened and he began to speak plainly.

Like the raising of Jairus's daughter, Jesus doesn't perform this miracle for the attention of the crowds. Instead, Christ pulls the deaf man aside, touches his ears and tongue, and asks his Father to heal him. Not only are the man's senses restored, but he's also granted the gift of clear speech.

The manner by which Jesus restores his speech seems odd: he touches the man's tongue with his own spit.

Some commentators believe that the people of

that day understood saliva to have healing properties and that Jesus was simply demonstrating his intention to heal. Others believe that by spitting on the infirmity, Jesus was showing his utter contempt for the condition that had caused this man so much misery. Whatever the case, the crowd was more amazed by the result than by the means.

> *36 Jesus commanded them not to tell anyone. But the more he did so, the more they kept talking about it. 37 People were overwhelmed with amazement. "He has done everything well," they said. "He even makes the deaf hear and the mute speak."*

This chapter concludes with a chorus of testimonies about Jesus. His miracles validate his message. His truth exposes their hypocrisy. His compassion transcends racial and religious differences.

Jesus does all things well.

PRAYER: Lord, if all it took were miracles to convince us of who you are, then everyone in Israel would have put their faith in you. Rather, you do miraculous things for those who come to you as Lord. Lord, I believe; help my unbelief. Make yourself known through my needs. Amen.

MARK 8

EPISODE 38

MORE THAN
FOUR THOUSAND FED

How many miracles will his disciples need to witness before they see Jesus for who he really is? How many signs and wonders will his skeptics require before they will lay aside their cynicism?

The answer is always "one more."

> *8:1 During those days another large crowd gathered. Since they had nothing to eat, Jesus called his disciples to him and said, 2 "I have compassion for these people; they have already been with me three days and have nothing to eat. 3 If I send them home hungry, they will collapse on the way, because some of them have come a long distance."*

This isn't the first time Jesus has challenged his men to provide for the overwhelming needs of a multitude. But on this occasion, the crowd has been encamped for three days, and some of them are literally too weak to walk home.

4 His disciples answered, "But where in this remote place can anyone get enough bread to feed them?"

What makes our hearts so slow to believe, yet so quick to surrender to the circumstances?

5 "How many loaves do you have?" Jesus asked. "Seven," they replied. 6 He told the crowd to sit down on the ground. When he had taken the seven loaves and given thanks, he broke them and gave them to his disciples to distribute to the people, and they did so. 7 They had a few small fish as well; he gave thanks for them also and told the disciples to distribute them.

Notice that Jesus' gratitude precedes God's provision. It's easy to be thankful for what we've already received, but it takes faith to be grateful in the presence of the problem.

8 The people ate and were satisfied. Afterward the disciples picked up seven basketfuls of broken pieces that were left over. 9 About four thousand were present. After he had sent them away, 10 he got into the boat with his disciples and went to the region of Dalmanutha.

PRAYER: Lord, this is the second time Mark records that you miraculously fed thousands of men, women and children. And yet, those closest to you seem clueless. Forgive me, Lord, when I am oblivious to all the ways and times you provide for my every need. Help me see your loving hand in even the direst of circumstances and trust you to care for me. Amen.

EPISODE 39

CHRIST NEEDS
NO MAN'S APPROVAL

8:11 The Pharisees came and began to question Jesus. To test him, they asked him for a sign from heaven. 12 He sighed deeply and said, "Why does this generation ask for a miraculous sign? Truly I tell you, no sign will be given to it." 13 Then he left them, got back into the boat and crossed to the other side.

Jesus and his men pull their boat ashore, only to encounter a group of skeptical Pharisees. The religious leaders insist that he perform a miracle to validate his teachings. Jesus is disappointed by their request and refuses to jump through their hoops.

Instead of giving them a sign, Christ sighs.

Those who call themselves "God's chosen" have seen plenty of miracles; and yet they ask for one more. Like their forefathers, supernatural miracles will never be enough to transform their hearts. Again, Christ refuses to yield to their authority. He simply turns around, steps back into his boat, and sails away.

PRAYER: Lord, help me understand that miracles are the result of faith, not doubt. You seek no one's approval or validation. Rather, you are the One who makes us righteous before your Father and validates us by your blood. So let my life be about your glory, not mine. Amen.

EPISODE 40

THE DISCIPLES ARE STILL OBLIVIOUS

8:14 The disciples had forgotten to bring bread, except for one loaf they had with them in the boat. 15 "Be careful," Jesus warned them. "Watch out for the yeast of the Pharisees and that of Herod."

Jesus knows that one day there will be a final showdown between himself, the Pharisees, and the Herodians. But it won't be today.

16 They discussed this with one another and said, "It is because we have no bread." 17 Aware of their discussion, Jesus asked them: "Why are you talking about having no bread? Do you still not see or understand? Are your hearts hardened? 18 Do you have eyes but fail to see, and ears but fail to hear? And don't you remember? 19 When I broke the five loaves for the five thousand, how many basketfuls of pieces did you pick up?" "Twelve," they replied. 20 "And when I broke the seven loaves for the four thousand, how many basketfuls of pieces did you pick up?" They answered, "Seven." 21 He said to them, "Do you still not understand?"

Israel's religious and political leaders oppose Jesus. His closest followers seem oblivious to what he's trying to teach them. It's no wonder that he sighs deeply at the Pharisee's hard-heartedness and is visibly frustrated by his disciples' hard-headedness. But rather than simply giving them the answer, Christ keeps asking them the question.

PRAYER: Lord, thank you for never giving up on those you love. Like a patient parent, you teach us the same lessons time and again until the truth begins to break through, and we apprehend it. You use every circumstance and challenge to reveal yourself to us. Help me recognize the truth, so that my mind may be renewed and my heart set free. Amen.

EPISODE 41

JESUS HEALS PRIVATELY

8:22 They came to Bethsaida, and some people brought a blind man and begged Jesus to touch him. 23 He took the blind man by the hand and led him outside the village. When he had spit on the man's eyes and put his hands on him, Jesus asked, "Do you see anything?" 24 He looked up and said, "I see people; they look like trees walking around." 25 Once more Jesus put his hands on the man's eyes. Then his eyes were opened, his sight was restored, and he saw everything clearly. 26 Jesus sent him home, saying, "Don't even go into the village."

Jesus doesn't do tricks for the crowds. Rather, he takes this blind man aside privately to heal him. The Son of God takes him by the hand, leading him out of a lifetime of darkness into the light. It's noteworthy that the restoration of this man's vision comes in two stages, rather than in one miraculous moment. This reminds us that we can't always predict how or when God will choose to work in our lives.

Christ meets the physical needs of people to demonstrate that he loves them and wants to meet their deepest spiritual needs as well. Unfortunately, people misinterpreted these miracles as a means to their own ends rather than as a sign of the coming kingdom of God. The clamoring crowds actually became a hindrance to Jesus' mission of revealing his Father's plan. So after Jesus heals this blind man, he tells him to avoid going back into the village so that he won't create a public sensation.

PRAYER: Lord, help me understand that—although your greatest work was done on a hillside overlooking a city—much of your healing goes unseen by the multitudes. You take each of us aside and meet our individual needs. Your blood, tears, and spit redeem and restore our bodies, minds, and spirits. Your miracles may be mysterious, but your love is so obvious. Thank you. Amen.

EPISODE 42

"WHO DO YOU SAY I AM?"

8:27 Jesus and his disciples went on to the villages around Caesarea Philippi. On the way he asked them, "Who do people say I am?" 28 They replied, "Some say John the Baptist; others say Elijah; and still others, one of the prophets." 29 "But what about you?" he asked. "Who do you say I am?" Peter answered, "You are the Messiah." 30 Jesus warned them not to tell anyone about him.

Peter's confession is a breakthrough moment for Jesus and his men. Although the Twelve have left everything to follow him, they're often confused and fearful. But these months of ambiguity and anxiety are punctuated by moments of transforming clarity. This is one of them.

It's not enough for Jesus' followers to acknowledge what other people say about him; Jesus wants to know what they believe. Peter's response hits the nail on the head: "You are the Messiah."

This simple confession embodies all the hopes and dreams of a nation enslaved and impoverished by political and spiritual oppression. This statement is clear and unequivocal, allowing no room for doubt or misinterpretation.

But more than being God's deliverer for the Jewish people, Peter's profession of Christ is a deeply personal one. It's as if he's saying, *"Jesus, you're the embodiment of all of my hopes and dreams. You're my Messiah, the One who can deliver me from slavery and poverty to freedom and sufficiency."*

Christ then warns them not to broadcast this message. That time would come soon enough; but it wasn't at hand. The Jews were looking for a messiah to overthrow their oppressors and restore Israel to its former glory. But that would be far too small an outcome for Jesus' mission. Rather, in a little while, he will set his face toward Jerusalem—and ultimately Calvary—to accomplish nothing less than the restoration of all humanity and the transformation of heaven and earth.

PRAYER: Jesus, this is the most important question I will ever answer. If I confess you as the Christ, the Son of the Living God, then every other thing in my life changes priority. You become the One who gives everything else its meaning. You become the context for my life. This changes everything. So change me, Lord. Amen.

EPISODE 43

JESUS TEACHES PLAINLY

Everything Jesus has done and said has led his disciples to the realization that he is the Christ, the long-awaited Messiah. And now that his men are beginning to see him clearly, Jesus can begin telling them plainly about his true mission.

8:31 He then began to teach them that the Son of Man must suffer many things and be rejected by the elders, chief priests and teachers of the law, and that he must be killed and after three days rise again.

Jesus has come to teach, preach, heal and liberate. But more than any of these, he has come to die for the sins of humanity. The perfect Son of God steps into the shoes of every man and woman who will ever live so that he can assume the penalty for their willful rebellion against God's plan and purpose. Like a perfect sacrificial lamb slain upon the Temple altar, his life will be taken and his blood poured out to pay the price for our sins.

His rejection by religious leaders proves the irrelevancy of religion. His condemnation by the teachers of the Law proves the futility of legalism. His defiance of death and hell demonstrate his Lordship over life itself.

> *32 He spoke plainly about this, and Peter took him aside and began to rebuke him. 33 But when Jesus turned and looked at his disciples, he rebuked Peter. "Get behind me, Satan!" he said. "You do not have in mind the things of God, but merely human concerns."*

Peter is bewildered. Only a few moments ago, he has rightly confessed Jesus as God's chosen Messiah. But rather than ushering in his kingdom, Jesus now seems bent on suicide. Peter exclaims, *"No, Lord!"*— two words that hardly belong in the same phrase. Jesus rebukes him as if he were Satan himself because his Father's plan will require real suffering, real sacrifice, and real death.

PRAYER: Lord, your ways are not our ways. The path you chose for yourself isn't the path I would have chosen. Likewise, the road to which you've called me may be confounding and challenging—until I look back and realize that your plans are perfect. Help me to see with the eyes of faith instead of fear. Help me to trust you: the One who rejected Satan's easy compromise and pressed hard to the cross for my blessing and your Father's glory. Amen.

EPISODE 44

GAINING THE WORLD BUT LOSING OUR SOULS

8:34 Then he called the crowd to him along with his disciples and said: "Whoever wants to be my disciple must deny themselves and take up their cross and follow me. 35 For whoever wants to save their life will lose it, but whoever loses their life for me and for the gospel will save it."

Christ foretells the means of his execution: a brutal crucifixion upon a Roman cross. There will be no shortcuts, no bending of the rules, and no lowering of the bar. Jesus will have to die to redeem us.

And we will have to be crucified with Christ in order to experience the redemption his sacrifice will purchase.

Jesus tells the crowd that anyone who wants to live in his kingdom must be willing to die to the world and its treasures. The choice is simple and direct, even for people in our day and age:

36 "What good is it for someone to gain the whole world, yet forfeit their soul? 37 Or what can anyone give in exchange for their soul? 38 If anyone is ashamed of me and my words in this adulterous and sinful generation, the Son of Man will be ashamed of them when he comes in his Father's glory with the holy angels."

This isn't mere metaphor and symbolism. Christ declares that one day he'll return in the unveiled power of his Father's glory, accompanied by a fierce angelic army to judge the living and the dead.

On that day, Jesus will confront each of us with the same question he asked Peter, *"But what about you...who do you say that I am?"*

And answer we will.

PRAYER: Lord, I admit that I'm tempted to live for my benefit rather than for your glory. Forgive me when I confess you with my lips but deny you with my heart. I choose to submit my will to yours. Crucify my old sin-filled self and resurrect your new creation in me so that I might live boldly for you until you come—or until I go. Amen.

MARK 9

EPISODE 45

HIS SOON-COMING KINGDOM

9:1 And he said to them, "I tell you the truth, some who are standing here will not taste death before they see the kingdom of God come with power."

In a matter of weeks, many within the sound of Jesus' voice will experience the greatest miracle the world has ever known: the bodily resurrection of a man who's been executed and entombed. The earth will shake, the large stone that seals his grave will roll away, and an angel will proclaim, *"He is risen."* And yet, the religiously obstinate, the politically vested, and the philosophically skeptical will continue to reject his Lordship.

Then, forty days following Jesus' ascension into heaven, some of those standing in this very crowd will experience the miracle of Pentecost, when God's Holy Spirit will descend to indwell and empower his followers to be his witnesses to the very ends of the earth.

And on still another day in the future, those born again into his eternal kingdom will witness Christ lead the armies of heaven in a final rout of the powers of political, spiritual, and material darkness.

After Jesus' resurrection and Pentecost, many early believers thought that Christ would return at any moment. As such, they became confused and discouraged when some of their brothers and sisters "tasted death" before his final advent. Like them, we should not be disheartened.

For the Jews, there was one simple test of whether a prophet was true or false. If what he said would happen happened, then everything else he prophesied was deemed trustworthy. Time and again, Christ's words were proven true. Prophecy after prophecy was fulfilled.

We therefore have every reason to trust that whatever has been left undone is closer than ever to being realized.

PRAYER: Like the early church, we cry, "Lord Jesus, quickly come!" Relieve our suffering, restore the broken, and recreate heaven and earth. Even so, empower us to proclaim your coming kingdom to those who still need to hear. Amen.

EPISODE 46

JESUS UNVEILS HIS GLORY

Even as Jesus alludes to this ultimate revelation of himself, three of his closest followers are about to be overwhelmed by a glimpse of his unveiled glory.

> *9:2 After six days Jesus took Peter, James and John with him and led them up a high mountain, where they were all alone. There he was transfigured before them. 3 His clothes became dazzling white, whiter than anyone in the world could bleach them.*

God reveals himself on mountains.

He gave Moses the Ten Commandments on Mount Sinai. The Lord called Abraham to sacrifice Isaac on a mountain. God displayed his power over the pagan prophets of Baal at Mount Carmel. The Jewish Temple, enshrining the Holy of Holies, was built on Mount Moriah in Jerusalem. Christ now unveils his supernatural nature on a mountaintop.

Peter, James, and John can barely trust their senses. Jesus' clothes become white, but not because of bleach. His whole body shimmers, but not because of the sun's reflection. Somehow, Christ's divine nature—cloaked for three decades in human flesh—is momentarily revealed. These three disciples, who have recently confessed Jesus' divinity with their mouths, now experience it with their eyes. Believing is seeing.

> *4 And there appeared before them Elijah and Moses, who were talking with Jesus.*

Mark underscores the fact that no one else is on the mountain with them when Elijah and Moses miraculously appear. These two Jewish patriarchs, gone for centuries, are called back from eternity to converse with Christ.

God does as he pleases. It pleases the Father for his Son to "talk things over" with Elijah and Moses. And it glorifies the Father to reveal the divine nature of his Son to Peter, James, and John.

> *5 Peter said to Jesus, "Rabbi, it is good for us to be here. Let us put up three shelters—one for you, one for Moses and one for Elijah." 6 (He did not know what to say, they were so frightened.) 7 Then a cloud appeared and enveloped them, and a voice came from the cloud: "This is my Son, whom I love. Listen to him!" 8 Suddenly, when they looked around, they no longer saw anyone with them except Jesus.*

Peter blurts out they should remain on the mountain and erect a trio of "tabernacles" where they can continue to worship these three holy men. But Jesus is more than just a prophet or patriarch. He's greater than the greatest men who have ever walked the earth.

The very next moment, the glory of the Lord manifests itself in a cloud from which God speaks. Yahweh himself addresses the disciples, expressing his love for his Son and commanding them to obey him as they would the Father. The testimony is complete. All has been said. Jesus is God's Son, the Messiah, Lord of heaven and earth.

> *9 As they were coming down the mountain, Jesus gave them orders not to tell anyone what they had seen until the Son of Man had risen from the dead. 10 They kept the matter to themselves, discussing what "rising from the dead" meant.*

PRAYER: Jesus, on that mountain, you weren't transformed into God; rather, you were transfigured into the God you already are. For you have been God from the beginning and will be God eternally. I am amazed how you temporarily laid aside your glory to bring us life through your death and resurrection. Because you are God, I will listen to you and bring you the glory you are due. Amen.

EPISODE 47

THE CROSS PRECEDES
THE CROWN

Even though Jesus has already revealed that he'll be persecuted, executed, and resurrected, his closest confidants still can't grasp what this means. But at least they are now asking good questions.

> *9:11 And they asked him, "Why do the teachers of the law say that Elijah must come first?" 12 Jesus replied, "To be sure, Elijah does come first, and restores all things. Why then is it written that the Son of Man must suffer much and be rejected? 13 But I tell you, Elijah has come, and they have done to him everything they wished, just as it is written about him."*

Peter, James, and John are trying to understand how Jesus' claim to be the Christ and their supernatural encounter with Moses and Elijah line up with Messianic prophecy. Jesus responds by telling them that Elijah's coming has been *figuratively fulfilled* in the person of John the Baptist, who heralded his arrival and laid the groundwork for everything to come. Furthermore, this prophecy was *literally fulfilled* in their presence as Elijah appeared with Christ on the mountaintop.

But that's not the main issue here...

The disciples are trying to piece together a timetable for when Jesus will inaugurate his kingdom—a kingdom in which they hope to exercise power and prestige.

Christ tells them not to get the cart before the horse. Yes, prophecy says that Elijah will precede Christ; but more importantly, Scripture foretells that Messiah will have to suffer and die before his kingdom comes in power. This is a message that Peter and the others will have a difficult time accepting until they are able to look back on it all from the perspective of Pentecost.

PRAYER: Lord, I am tempted to interpret Scripture to my own advantage and in my own interest. Instead, I pray that your Word would interpret me. Let your Spirit help me hear what you are saying so that I might do what you are doing. In your name I pray. Amen.

EPISODE 48

"I BELIEVE! HELP MY UNBELIEF!"

9:14 When they came to the other disciples, they saw a large crowd around them and the teachers of the law arguing with them. 15 As soon as all the people saw Jesus, they were overwhelmed with wonder and ran to greet him.

Jesus, Peter, James, and John come down the mountain to find the other disciples engaged in an encounter of their own.

16 "What are you arguing with them about?" he asked. 17 A man in the crowd answered, "Teacher, I brought you my son, who is possessed by a spirit that has robbed him of speech. 18 Whenever it seizes him, it throws him to the ground. He foams at the mouth, gnashes his teeth and becomes rigid. I asked your disciples to drive out the spirit, but they could not."

Like the myriads who have already brought their ailing friends and family members to Christ, this father hopes that Jesus can heal his son.

19 "You unbelieving generation," Jesus replied, "how long shall I stay with you? How long shall I put up with you? Bring the boy to me."

Though Christ is clearly vexed by his disciples' lack of faith, I imagine his criticism is spoken more in concerned frustration than in harsh condemnation. Like the teacher whose students still don't "get it" after repeated instruction, he begins the lesson again.

20 So they brought him. When the spirit saw Jesus, it immediately threw the boy into a convulsion. He fell to the ground and rolled around, foaming at the mouth.

This is more than a simple case of epilepsy: a devastating spiritual force is at work in this boy's life.

21 Jesus asked the boy's father, "How long has he been like this?" "From childhood," he answered. 22 "It has often thrown him into fire or water to kill him. But if you can do anything, take pity on us and help us." 23 "'If you can'?" said Jesus. "Everything is possible for him who believes." 24 Immediately the boy's father exclaimed, "I do believe; help me overcome my unbelief!"

Like this father, we are overwhelmed by our hopelessness and helplessness. We cry out to Christ, confessing that our faith is not up to challenge. Jesus hears us and becomes both the object of our belief and the very power we need to exercise that faith.

Our utter dependence is the only hope for our

total deliverance.

It's as if Jesus is saying, *"Now that you know you can't—I invite you to believe I can."* Make no mistake: it's not enough to trust in the power of positive thinking. Rather, we are called to place our faith in the person of Christ himself.

> *25 When Jesus saw that a crowd was running to the scene, he rebuked the impure spirit. "You deaf and mute spirit," he said, "I command you, come out of him and never enter him again." 26 The spirit shrieked, convulsed him violently and came out. The boy looked so much like a corpse that many said, "He's dead." 27 But Jesus took him by the hand and lifted him to his feet, and he stood up.*

Before another crowd can assemble, Jesus delivers the boy from the spiritual oppression that's also the source of his physical maladies. The process is so traumatic that it appears the child has actually died. But the next moment, Jesus helps the boy to his feet, whole and healthy.

> *28 After Jesus had gone indoors, his disciples asked him privately, "Why couldn't we drive it out?" 29 He replied, "This kind can come out only by prayer."*

Apparently, this spiritual battle was more demanding than some of the previous challenges the disciples had faced. As we will read in other gospel accounts, not every spiritual victory is won by "name-dropping." On the contrary, sometimes it will take hours, days, or even years of intercession before spiritual victory is achieved. And in every case, it will be eternity before each of us is made fully whole.

Each of us has a body, soul (mind and will) and spirit. What affects one part affects our whole. There can be no substantive healing of the body without restoration of the mind and redemption of the spirit. In this case, through no apparent fault of his own, this young boy was deaf, speechless, and prone to life-threatening seizures. His physical and emotional issues had a spiritual cause. Christ delivered this "demonized" child from the powers of darkness back into the arms of an imploring father.

What a wonderful picture of Jesus' entire mission.

PRAYER: Jesus, thank you for doing this same thing for me: destroying hell's hold upon my body, mind, and spirit and delivering me into your Father's embrace. Like that boy, I was virtually dead, but now I'm alive in you. Make me an agent of liberty, freeing those around me from their bondage and brokenness. In your name I pray. Amen.

EPISODE 49

STEALING AWAY WITH JESUS

9:30 They left that place and passed through Galilee. Jesus did not want anyone to know where they were, 31 because he was teaching his disciples. He said to them, "The Son of Man is going to be betrayed into the hands of men. They will kill him, and after three days he will rise." 32 But they did not understand what he meant and were afraid to ask him about it.

Christ withdraws from the masses to invest in his men. He pours himself into the Twelve so that each of them might pour themselves into dozens more. In this way, the kingdom will grow exponentially.

This is the third time Mark records Christ saying he will be crucified and then raised from the dead three days later. Though Jesus clearly predicts his fate, the apostles won't truly understand his words until after these events occur.

There are two important insights we can glean from this short passage.

First, sometimes it's more important to spend time with Christ than it is to minister to the masses. In this instance, Jesus intentionally keeps their whereabouts secret so that he can encourage and equip his disciples. Our public effectiveness will always be proportionate to the time we spend privately with Christ.

Second, the disciples lacked understanding because they were afraid to admit their ignorance and ask Jesus the hard questions. Like them, our pride and fear often keep us from realizing God's plan and purpose. When we bring our doubts and questions to Christ, we open the door to understanding and confidence. But until then, we will remain ignorant and afraid.

PRAYER: Lord, I'm overwhelmed by the thought that you actually want to spend time with me. Help me steal away with you so your Word can speak to my mind and your Spirit can speak to my heart. Deliver me from pride and fear and fill me with the confidence that comes from trust and understanding. Amen.

EPISODE 50

TRUE GREATNESS

9:33 They came to Capernaum. When he was in the house, he asked them, "What were you arguing about on the road?" 34 But they kept quiet because on the way they had argued about who was the greatest.

Jesus has surely overheard their conversation, but he wants them to "come clean" about their selfish ambitions. It's fascinating that the people who recounted these gospels were so transparent about their own foolishness and pride.

35 Sitting down, Jesus called the Twelve and said, "If anyone wants to be first, he must be the very last, and the servant of all." 36 He took a little child whom he had placed among them. Taking the child in his arms, he said to them, 37 "Whoever welcomes one of these little children in my name welcomes me; and whoever welcomes me does not welcome me but the one who sent me."

The Twelve are finally realizing that Jesus is God's Son and that his kingdom is truly at hand. But rather than humbly serving the Messiah who will lay down his life for them, they begin arguing about who will have the most prestigious positions in the new administration.

Jesus sits them down and tells them that the most honored citizens in his kingdom are those who put others first and themselves last. Likewise, the greatest are those who serve those with the least power and prestige. To illustrate, he stands a child before them and tells them that the way they love a child will demonstrate the way they love him.

This is a radical statement.

In Jesus' day, women and children had little status and were hardly valued as more than chattel, the personal property of the man of the household. Even today, millions of women and children around the world are denied basic human rights by men who oppress, exploit, and even enslave them. Perhaps nowhere else in Scripture is the loving character of God more clearly revealed than in how Christ speaks about his Father's compassion for children.

To God, every child is priceless: the born and the unborn, the young and the old. Although God is creator, provider, counselor and redeemer, his favorite name seems to be Father. He cherishes children and so do his true spiritual offspring. Jesus tells his followers that if they welcome a child in his name, they are actually welcoming him, and therefore welcoming the Father who sent him.

So what does it mean to "welcome" someone?

Middle Eastern culture placed a high value on the virtues of hospitality and charity. I was in Africa several years ago visiting a town decimated by the

HIV-AIDS virus, and yet the villagers killed and cooked one of their few goats in honor of our visit. Their hospitality was extravagant.

Throughout the Bible, people welcomed strangers and travelers into their homes, sharing the best of their meager provisions with them, thinking that they might be "entertaining angels unaware" (Hebrews 13:2). But welcoming a child in Jesus name is even better than entertaining an angel because we are welcoming the very Son of God!

In serving "the least of these," we are becoming merciful conduits of the same extravagant love God demonstrates toward us. In this sense, the welcoming a child in Jesus' name is as sacramental an act as the Lord's Supper or baptism.

PRAYER: Heavenly Father, help me learn to love your children as you do. Holy Son, help me welcome the little and the least as you did. Holy Spirit, convict my heart when I aspire to greatness as the world defines it. Instead, empty and empower me to love and serve so that the world might see you in me. Amen.

EPISODE 51

WHO'S WITH US (AND WHO'S NOT)?

9:38 "Teacher," said John, "we saw someone driving out demons in your name and we told him to stop, because he was not one of us."

As word of the Messiah spreads, people outside Jesus' immediate circle begin to preach and heal in his name. He tells his men not to be threatened by this development, because henceforth the world will be dividing itself into those who are for Christ and those who are against him.

39 "Do not stop him," Jesus said. "For no one who does a miracle in my name can in the next moment say anything bad about me, 40 for whoever is not against us is for us.

In another gospel, Jesus says, *"If you're not for me, you're against me"* (Matthew 12:30). But in this situation he says, "If you're not against us, you're for us." Both are true because there's no middle ground when it involves allegiance to Christ and his kingdom.

41 Truly I tell you, anyone who gives you a cup of water in my name because you belong to the Messiah will certainly not lose their reward.

Just as those who welcome a child in Jesus name will be blessed, those who demonstrate even the smallest act of kindness toward Christ's ambassadors will be rewarded as though they are doing it for him.

It's as if Jesus is saying, *"My kingdom is bigger than you suppose. It doesn't matter whether or not they're on your side as long as they're on my side."*

Before leaving this topic, Jesus re-emphasizes his concern for the welfare of children:

42 "If anyone causes one of these little ones—those who believe in me--to stumble, it would be better for them if a large millstone were hung around their neck and they were thrown into the sea.

Jesus warns that actions can have profound consequences. Those who extend even the smallest blessing to his children will be blessed. Conversely, people who harm the smallest and most vulnerable of his flock will regret it. Those who really know Christ will be known by both his power and his love.

PRAYER: Lord, give me charity toward believers who aren't just like me. Help me be thrilled when your name is praised and your children are blessed. Likewise, let me be careful not to cause others to stumble—especially the little, the lowly and the lost. In your name I pray. Amen.

EPISODE 52

AMPUTATION VS. REGENERATION

J esus then challenges us to reject anything that might keep us from following him wholeheartedly.

> *9:43 If your hand causes you to stumble, cut it off. It is better for you to enter life maimed than with two hands to go into hell, where the fire never goes out. 45 And if your foot causes you to stumble, cut it off. It is better for you to enter life crippled than to have two feet and be thrown into hell. 47 And if your eye causes you to stumble, pluck it out. It is better for you to enter the kingdom of God with one eye than to have two eyes and be thrown into hell, 48 where '"the worms that eat them do not die, and the fire is not quenched.'*

This passage has been misunderstood by the faithful and faithless alike.

If we interpret Christ's words literally, disciples would maim themselves for the sake of the gospel. A literal understanding of this section falls far short of its true meaning. In fact, cutting off our hands and gouging out our eyes are unbiblical and ineffective remedies to sin.

What we touch, where we go, and what we see are first functions of our hearts, then our bodies. By using hyperbole, Christ highlights the absurdity of pursuing physical solutions to what are essentially spiritual issues. Jesus requires something even more extreme than self-mutilation: we must die to ourselves for the sake of his lordship.

The answer is not amputation, but regeneration.

We need new hearts ruled by Christ. In turn, our new hearts can rule our bodies in a way that truly honors God. We can't take our sin with us to heaven, so why should we abide with it here on earth? Without true repentance, a life spent on sin will result in an eternity spent without God.

Christ uses metaphorical language to describe hell as a condition of continuous decay and unquenchable fire, much like the garbage dump that burned outside the city gates of Jerusalem day in and day out. A metaphor doesn't mean something is mythical; rather, it means that literal language cannot adequately describe it. Hell is more real than words can express, and should be avoided at all costs.

PRAYER: Heavenly Father, help me understand that you hate sin so much because you love us so much. Because of your immeasurable love, you sent your only Son to suffer and die on my behalf. How can I allow the sin for which Christ suffered and died to remain in my life? Sanctify and transform my body and mind so that the words of my mouth and the meditations of my heart will be acceptable in your sight. Amen.

EPISODE 53

PURPOSE IN THE PAIN

9:49 Everyone will be salted with fire. 50 "Salt is good, but if it loses its saltiness, how can you make it salty again? Have salt in yourselves, and be at peace with each other."

Jesus now joins the metaphors of fire and salt. Although he has just described the eternal flames of hell, in these verses he declares that all of us will experience the refining fire of trials.

Trials are inevitable. Even though most of us would prefer to avoid them, the Lord uses them for his glory and our good.

If our lives aren't anchored in God, he uses life's trials to help us realize our own inadequacy that we might come to faith in him. For those of us who have chosen to follow Christ, he uses the challenges of life as a furnace to help burn away anything that's not eternal—leaving us more like him. Our faith in God grows when we learn to trust him through circumstances beyond our control.

This is ultimately God's purpose for us: that this refining process will produce a precious and pure element—a salt—that will bring our lives true meaning and profound peace. Christ tells us that this transcendent serenity will not only pervade our inner lives but also positively transform our relationships with one another.

PRAYER: Lord, it's so difficult for me to see your hand in life's hardships. Help me trust that you can use even the worst things for your glory and my good. For you have purposed that my sanctification be accomplished through the refiner's fire. So not my will but yours be done. Amen.

MARK 10

EPISODE 54

A TRICK QUESTION
ABOUT DIVORCE

10:1 Jesus then left that place and went into the region of Judea and across the Jordan. Again crowds of people came to him, and as was his custom, he taught them.

The headwaters of the Jordan River are in northern Israel. From there, the river runs more than 150 miles due south into the Sea of Galilee until it eventually empties into the Dead Sea. The region of Judea sits on the western bank of the Dead Sea, a body of water almost nine times saltier than the ocean.

2 Some Pharisees came and tested him by asking, "Is it lawful for a man to divorce his wife?"

The Pharisees are on a mission to discredit and destroy Jesus. Their plan is to bait him into blaspheming God and disparaging the Mosaic Law. But they don't realize that Jesus would never dishonor his heavenly Father or contradict his Word. In fact, Christ says that he's come to fulfill the Law and the Prophets (Matthew 5:17-19). He answers their question by appealing directly to Scripture itself.

> *3 "What did Moses command you?" he replied. 4 They said, "Moses permitted a man to write a certificate of divorce and send her away." 5 "It was because your hearts were hard that Moses wrote you this law," Jesus replied.*

Marriage was sacred among the Jews and therefore divorce was generally prohibited. But men devised ways around the spirit of the Law while ostensibly keeping its letter. An unscrupulous husband who wanted a divorce might accuse his wife of adultery, an offense punishable by death. If his wife fled--or worse, if she were stoned to death—he would be free to remarry. To prevent this travesty, Moses allowed a husband, under certain circumstances, to divorce his wife by giving her a certificate of annulment. This document legally terminated the marriage and allowed both parties to remarry. This was especially critical for women, who were economically disadvantaged and might otherwise resort to vagrancy or prostitution if they were prohibited from remarrying. Although this was an obvious concession to men's callousness, annulment became more and more common, so that a husband could divorce his wife over anything she did which might displease him.

The Pharisees know this issue is controversial and that Jesus' answer will make him unpopular with some segment of the people. But Christ is not concerned with pleasing men; rather, his response reflects his Father's eternal purpose. His answer causes the self-righteous to be condemned by the very Law they allegedly obey.

PRAYER: Father, convict my heart when I use your Law for my own selfish ends instead of your godly ones. Help me understand that your ways are higher than mine and that you desire obedience rather than sacrifice. I realize that your forbearance and mercy are meant for my redemption, not my excess. So give me a heart that seeks and honors you. Amen.

EPISODE 55

GOD'S DESIGN FOR MARRIAGE

10:6 "But at the beginning of creation God 'made them male and female.' 7 'For this reason a man will leave his father and mother and be united to his wife, 8 and the two will become one flesh.' So they are no longer two, but one. 9 Therefore what God has joined together, let no one separate."

Jesus cites God's clear design for marriage as recorded in Genesis, a book authored in large part by Moses. Christ considers Moses' words to be true and authoritative, as should we. There are three basic principles in this passage.

First, Jesus plainly defines marriage as the union between one man and one woman. Any alternative defies God's plan and purpose.

Second, marriage involves a profound "one flesh" mystery. This intimacy is far more than physical; so much that two autonomous people actually become one in heart. This union hints at the mystery of the Trinity where the three distinct personalities of Father, Son, and Spirit exist as one divine essence.

Third, God himself is the agent of this union. His

involvement makes marriage sacred and indivisible without his permission. Marriage is not meant to be a mere civil contract between a man and a woman. Rather, biblical marriage involves an authoritative third party, God, who joins husband and wife together in this permanent, lifelong covenant.

The Bible recounts how humanity ignored God's plan for marriage by practicing polygamy, adultery, homosexuality, and divorce. We reasoned that we'd be happier if we followed our own hearts. But we couldn't comprehend how deeply our hearts had been corrupted by sin.

Jesus doesn't sanction our self-indulgence. Instead, he takes this opportunity to restore the institution of marriage to the sacred position it has held in his Father's heart since the beginning of time.

> *10 When they were in the house again, the disciples asked Jesus about this. 11 He answered, "Anyone who divorces his wife and marries another woman commits adultery against her. 12 And if she divorces her husband and marries another man, she commits adultery."*

Jesus is not being judgmental or hateful. On the contrary, in the coming days Christ will lay down his life for each and every sin committed by each and every one of us. He will bear the punishment rightly due us for our treason against God. As such, he's justified in calling us to live lives in obedience to his Father.

PRAYER: Father, tune my heart to your plans and purposes for me. Help me love your Law more than my lawlessness. Empower me by your Holy Spirit to reject the world's definition of love and marriage and to be defined by your design. Let me live and love in a way that honors you and those closest to me. Amen.

EPISODE 56

THE KINGDOM
BELONGS TO KIDS

10:13 People were bringing little children to Jesus for him to place his hands on them, but the disciples rebuked them. 14 When Jesus saw this, he was indignant. He said to them, "Let the little children come to me, and do not hinder them, for the kingdom of God belongs to such as these. 15 I tell you the truth, anyone who will not receive the kingdom of God like a little child will never enter it." 16 And he took the children in his arms, placed his hands on them and blessed them.

It's noteworthy that Mark records this episode about children immediately after Christ's discourse on divorce. Our modern culture is filled with the consequences of failed relationships: broken homes, single parents, and blended families.

The solution?

The Son of God calls us to bring our kids to him and for us to come to him as children do.

To Jesus' disciples, children are a distracting

nuisance. But to Christ, children are the very embodiment of his Father's kingdom. Jesus is indignant, perhaps even outraged, at his disciples' insensitivity. *No! Bring them to me in their helplessness and dependence! This is what it looks like to come as a child to my Father!*

Imagine being the parent of a child held and blessed by Jesus! What a moment when you realize that the very Son of God is cradling your baby!

Today, Christ continues to reach out to embrace the children of the world through the open arms of Christians. Likewise, parents can come to know our Savior through the way we supply the needs of their children. The love of our Father can be profoundly demonstrated through our compassion for their kids.

PRAYER: Lord, give me your heart for children. Help me be more intentional about caring for the kids you have put around me as well as your children around the world. Let me invest in their future as others have invested in mine. Use children to teach me what it means to come to you as a child. Amen.

EPISODE 57

INHERITING ETERNAL LIFE

10:17 As Jesus started on his way, a man ran up to him and fell on his knees before him. "Good teacher," he asked, "what must I do to inherit eternal life?" 18 "Why do you call me good?" Jesus answered. "No one is good—except God alone.

Imagine the scene: a fairly well-to-do man runs up to Jesus, falls at his feet, and asks what he must do to live forever.

But that's not exactly what he says. Rather, he asks, "Good teacher, what must I do to inherit eternal life?"

His words are as rich as he seems to be.

First, he realizes that Christ has extraordinary authority in this matter. He addresses Jesus as "good teacher." This isn't just pandering lip-service, for he's speaking these words from his knees.

Second, he realizes that eternal life is something he can't acquire through his wealth or position. Because he's been raised in a religious culture, he assumes that his eternal "reward" is somehow connected with his earthly deeds. He just wants to know what to "do."

Third, even though he assumes that eternal life is acquired by works, he uses the word "inherit" in his question. As a rule, to *inherit* means that the rightful owner must die and bequeath his property to another. Ironically, the man is correct. The rightful owner of eternal life will have to die in order to "will" it to us.

Jesus responds with a question of his own: "Why do you call me good?" He isn't being humble. Rather, he's trying to see if the guy truly understands to whom he is speaking.

Christ turns this man's salutation into a syllogism: *If no one is good except God, and if you have characterized me as good, then either I am not good—or I am God.*

Eternal life can't be earned by human effort. Rather, it can only be inherited by God's true children upon the death of his one and only Son. And yet, as Jesus will later reveal, there's a condition to receiving this inheritance: full faith and trust in him that will be evidenced by how we live.

PRAYER: Jesus, thank you for dying in my place so that I might inherit all you have. Forgive me when I try to earn my place in your kingdom. Likewise, forgive me when my deeds betray that I have confessed you as Lord of all. Amen.

EPISODE 58

POSSESSED BY POSSESSIONS

10:19 "You know the commandments: 'You shall not murder, you shall not commit adultery, you shall not steal, you shall not give false testimony, you shall not defraud, honor your father and mother.' 20 "Teacher," he declared, "all these I have kept since I was a boy."

Christ's detractors hope that he will somehow blaspheme God or disparage the Mosaic Law. To their chagrin, Jesus reaffirms these commandments as God's standard for righteous living. And yet, he reveals that it's possible to keep the letter of the Law while ignoring its true intent.

Jesus knows that this man's affections are tangled up in his possessions. What Christ will require of him flows from God's profound compassion for him—and the world.

21 Jesus looked at him and loved him. "One thing you lack," he said. "Go, sell everything you have and give to the poor, and you will have treasure in heaven. Then come, follow me." 22 At this the man's face fell. He went away sad, because he had great wealth.

The God of Creation demands that we look to

him exclusively for our identity, security, and eternity. It's impossible for us to have "no other gods" when we trust in created stuff more than we do in the Creator himself. Not only are we tempted to find our self-worth and self-sufficiency in our possessions, but the hoarding of wealth prevents us from being generous to those around us who are suffering.

Jesus could have commanded this man to destroy all his riches, but that isn't God's heart. The Lord blesses us so that we might bless others, especially those who have little or nothing. This man's life—though outwardly characterized by righteous living—was inwardly defined by idolatry against God and indifference toward his fellow man. That's why Jesus instructs him to sell everything he has and give the proceeds to the poor.

It's important to understand that it's not the disposition of his possessions that qualifies him for heaven. Rather, his unwillingness to obey shows that this man treasured his wealth more than obeying God.

He has disqualified himself.

Christ calls us to put God and others before ourselves. How we handle our money and possessions will persuasively testify where our priorities lie.

PRAYER: Father in heaven, you are the source of every good and perfect gift. Let me recognize and appreciate your provision by treating everything as yours. Help me not be defined or distracted by things. Make me a good steward of that with which you've blessed me, understanding that you intend to bless others through me for your glory. Empower me to be generous to others—not just out of my abundance, but from my poverty as well. Amen.

EPISODE 59

HOW WEALTH WARS
WITH OUR SOULS

10:23 Jesus looked around and said to his disciples, "How hard it is for the rich to enter the kingdom of God!" 24 The disciples were amazed at his words. But Jesus said again, "Children, how hard it is to enter the kingdom of God! 25 It is easier for a camel to go through the eye of a needle than for someone who is rich to enter the kingdom of God." 26 The disciples were even more amazed, and said to each other, "Who then can be saved?" 27 Jesus looked at them and said, "With man this is impossible, but not with God; all things are possible with God."

Wealth has an animating power of its own, so much that the Bible uses a special word, *mammon*, to describe its capacity to corrupt our hearts. Even modest prosperity can produce a sense of entitlement, invulnerability, and pride which wars against Christ's call to generosity, unselfishness, and humility. Jesus warns that, without divine intervention, we may gain the world for a lifetime but lose our souls for eternity.

Our insatiable pursuit of mammon can blind us to how financially blessed we really are. Most of us act like we're barely getting by—even though we have cars in our garages and roofs on our air-conditioned homes and leftovers in our refrigerators. And yet, more than a billion people in our world today don't have access to basic food and water needs.

North Americans comprise about five percent of the world's population, yet we control over a quarter of the world's wealth. According to a United Nations University study, in the year 2000, the richest one percent of the world's adults owned 40% of its assets and the richest 10% of adults owned 85% of the world's wealth. The bottom half of the planet's adult population possessed barely one percent of its global assets.

There's a huge disparity between the "haves" and the "have not's," yet the Gospel doesn't call for a legalistic realignment of wealth. Rather, Christ calls for a radical realignment of our hearts.

This transformation will create an understanding of wealth as a means to help deliver God's children from hunger, disease, ignorance, and despair. Time and again, Jesus tells his followers that this kind of living persuades the world that God is real and the gospel is true.

PRAYER: Christ, when it was impossible for me to earn my own salvation, you became poor so that I could enjoy the riches of your Kingdom. Now that I belong to you, destroy the power that mammon has over me by helping me give my wealth away.

Instead of passing the responsibility to others or to the government, give me the joy of caring for the poor and disenfranchised. Help me learn to be as impossibly generous to others as you have been to me. Amen.

EPISODE 60

GAINING WHAT
WE CANNOT LOSE

10:28 Peter said to him, "We have left everything to follow you!" 29 "I tell you the truth," Jesus replied, "no one who has left home or brothers or sisters or mother or father or children or fields for me and the gospel 30 will fail to receive a hundred times as much in this present age: homes, brothers, sisters, mothers, children and fields—along with persecutions--and in the age to come, eternal life. 31 But many who are first will be last, and the last first."

Peter looks at the rich young man walking away from the Giver of Eternal Life and blurts out, *"Lord, we've done what he couldn't—or wouldn't—do."*

Jesus responds that true discipleship will cost us everything we once thought priceless: where we live, whom we love, and what we do. His words are a far cry from much of today's prosperity gospel that teaches that faith in Christ will get us everything we want. The opposite is actually true: following Jesus will cost us everything we have.

170

But once our hands and hearts are empty of things we can't keep, God can fill them with things that can never be taken away. No matter what we forfeit for Christ in this life, it will pale in comparison with the exponential benefits we will receive as his children.

Jesus is clear that these blessings will not be fully realized until his kingdom fully comes. In the meantime, he warns us to expect hardships because of our status as members of his family.

He then underscores this principle by saying that those who are on top in this world will be on the bottom in the next—and vice versa. So we should not assume that worldly wealth is a blessing from God. Maybe it is; maybe it isn't.

What really matters is living lives wholly committed to Christ and his kingdom.

PRAYER: Convict my heart when I pursue the things of this world more than the things of the next. Help me hold all things lightly, being confident that you hold me tightly. Let me lay up treasures in heaven, leaving behind what I cannot keep to receive what I cannot lose. Amen.

EPISODE 61

WITH FULL FOREKNOWLEDGE

10:32 They were on their way up to Jerusalem, with Jesus leading the way, and the disciples were astonished, while those who followed were afraid. Again he took the Twelve aside and told them what was going to happen to him. 33 "We are going up to Jerusalem," he said, "and the Son of Man will be betrayed to the chief priests and teachers of the law. They will condemn him to death and will hand him over to the Gentiles, 34 who will mock him and spit on him, flog him and kill him. Three days later he will rise."

Jesus begins his final trek toward Jerusalem. Those closest to him continue to be astonished. Those outside his inner circle fear what will happen when he arrives.

But Christ is undeterred.

Once again, he reveals the details of his upcoming ordeal to the Twelve. His death will be at the hands of both the Jews and the Gentiles. His resurrection will be for the whole world. No one will take his life from him; rather, he'll lay it down willingly with clear knowledge of all that will transpire.

And yet, knowing what will happen does not make it any easier.

PRAYER: Lord, let me never labor under the fallacy that you were a mere martyr. No. From the beginning, your mission has been to seek and save your lost world by revealing yourself as its Messiah and laying down your life as its Savior. Thank you for your never-wavering love. Amen.

EPISODE 62

POWER VS. GREATNESS

10:35 Then James and John, the sons of Zebedee, came to him. "Teacher," they said, "we want you to do for us whatever we ask."

Have you ever heard children asking their parents to promise to do something for them before they'll say what it is? James and John are using this same tactic with Jesus.

But like a compassionate parent, Christ uses their naïve and self-serving question to create a teachable moment for all of his closest men.

36 "What do you want me to do for you?" he asked. 37 They replied, "Let one of us sit at your right and the other at your left in your glory." 38 "You don't know what you are asking," Jesus said. "Can you drink the cup I drink or be baptized with the baptism I am baptized with?" 39 "We can," they answered. Jesus said to them, "You will drink the cup I drink and be baptized with the baptism I am baptized with, 40 but to sit at my right or left is not for me to grant. These places belong to those for whom they have been prepared."

41 When the ten heard about this, they became indignant with James and John. 42 Jesus called them together and said, "You know that those who are regarded as rulers of the Gentiles lord it over them, and their high officials exercise authority over them. 43 Not so with you. Instead, whoever wants to become great among you must be your servant, 44 and whoever wants to be first must be slave of all. 45 For even the Son of Man did not come to be served, but to serve, and to give his life as a ransom for many."

Jesus reminds us that in our world's system, the strong and the rich dominate the weak and the poor. But in Christ's kingdom, greatness does not come by power or privilege. Rather, it's realized through humility and service. Jesus says, *"Watch my example: I have come to offer my very life for all who will accept my sacrifice."*

And so they continue their journey from the western bank of the Jordan River east through Jericho and toward Jerusalem, the place where our ultimate ransom will be paid.

PRAYER: Jesus, convict me when I try to scheme my way to power and position. Instead, let me simply follow in your footsteps, love those you love, and lay down my life for those you came to save. Deliver me from the arrogance of entitlement by giving me your servant's heart. Amen.

EPISODE 63

A BLIND MAN SEES

10:46 Then they came to Jericho. As Jesus and his disciples, together with a large crowd, were leaving the city, a blind man, Bartimaeus (which means "Son of Timaeus"), was sitting by the roadside begging. 47 When he heard that it was Jesus of Nazareth, he began to shout, "Jesus, Son of David, have mercy on me!" 48 Many rebuked him and told him to be quiet, but he shouted all the more, "Son of David, have mercy on me!" 49 Jesus stopped and said, "Call him." So they called to the blind man, "Cheer up! On your feet! He's calling you." 50 Throwing his cloak aside, he jumped to his feet and came to Jesus. 51 "What do you want me to do for you?" Jesus asked him. The blind man said, "Rabbi, I want to see." 52 "Go," said Jesus, "your faith has healed you." Immediately he received his sight and followed Jesus along the road.

In contrast to a rich young ruler who is healthy, educated and influential--Jesus now encounters a poor man who is blind, illiterate, and powerless. And yet, the son of Timaeus has the uncommon sense to doggedly cry out to Christ and beg for mercy.

Perhaps this is a wonderful definition of faith:

crying out to God in our darkness, believing that he will do something.

It's telling that the crowd is more interested in what Jesus could do for them than in what he could do for the less fortunate. In spite of their rebuke, Christ hears the plea of this disruptive beggar.

Bartimaeus receives his sight and so much more.

PRAYER: Son of David, have mercy on me! I cry to you in my distress, even when those around me discourage me from doing so. I fling off my coverings and run to you. Without you, I am desperate, blind and helpless. In you, I have everything I need. Thank you. Amen.

MARK 11

EPISODE 64

ON A BORROWED COLT

11:1 As they approached Jerusalem and came to Bethphage and Bethany at the Mount of Olives, Jesus sent two of his disciples, 2 saying to them, "Go to the village ahead of you, and just as you enter it, you will find a colt tied there, which no one has ever ridden. Untie it and bring it here. 3 If anyone asks you, 'Why are you doing this?' tell him, 'The Lord needs it and will send it back here shortly.' "

These two villages are on the eastern outskirts of Jerusalem on the road west from Jericho. Rather than flaunting his divine right as Messiah by parading into Jerusalem with swords and horsemen, Jesus will ride into Israel's capital on the back of an unbroken, borrowed colt.

4 They went and found a colt outside in the street, tied at a doorway. As they untied it, 5 some people standing there asked, "What are you doing, untying that colt?" 6 They answered as Jesus had told them to, and the people let them go.

Again, Jesus demonstrates his foreknowledge of circumstances. The events that will unfold before him are entirely by God's design.

PRAYER: Lord, I take confidence in the fact that you existed before time, know everything that has ever happened, and know everything that ever will happen. I can trust you with every detail of my life. Amen.

EPISODE 65

TRIUMPHANTLY ENTERING JERUSALEM

11:7 When they brought the colt to Jesus and threw their cloaks over it, he sat on it. 8 Many people spread their cloaks on the road, while others spread branches they had cut in the fields. 9 Those who went ahead and those who followed shouted, "Hosanna!" "Blessed is he who comes in the name of the Lord!" 10 "Blessed is the coming kingdom of our father David!" "Hosanna in the highest!"

Jerusalem is packed with faithful Jews who have come from all over the world to observe the Passover Feast and celebrate their liberation from Egyptian slavery more than a thousand years earlier.

Every Jewish child can recite the story of the Passover:

Due to a famine in the land, Jacob and his family relocate to Egypt where God has made his son, Joseph, the Pharaoh's second in command. But decades pass and the Jewish population multiplies so much that the Egyptians enslave them out of fear they will become too powerful. The Lord raises up Moses to deliver his people, but the new Pharaoh ignores both Moses' pleas and God's plagues.

So God instructs every Hebrew family to kill a lamb and brush its blood on the doorposts of their homes. That night, after each Jewish household has eaten the cooked lamb and other ritual foods, the Lord strikes down the firstborn of each family and flock in Egypt. Only those homes covered by the blood of the lamb are "passed over." This final plague convinces Pharaoh to release the Jews from their captivity. But even as Moses and the Israelites flee, Pharaoh changes his mind and sends his armies to recapture his nation of slaves. Pinned against the Red Sea, God miraculously delivers the Jews by parting the waters so that they can escape. Undaunted, Pharaoh's army pursues them into the seabed. The Lord then releases the floods to destroy the force that has oppressed his people for centuries.

Now, more than a thousand years later, the Jews are in captivity again. The Roman Empire has a stranglehold on their country, their economy, and even their religion. When the Jews gather in Jerusalem to commemorate the Passover, it's more than a placid religious observance. They're begging God to once again deliver them from bondage. They're pleading for God to restore Israel to its glory. They're expecting God's Messiah.

For the past three years, thousands have seen Jesus preach and tens of thousands have heard about his miracles. Could this be the man? Could this be the moment?

In what must have threatened the Romans and terrified the Pharisees, the main highway into

Jerusalem is now pulsing with Messianic fervor. Throngs are shouting nationalistic slogans and putting their coats on the road to make a way for their coming king. They cut palm fronds from nearby trees and wave them at Jesus as they have seen the servants of the rich and powerful do to for their masters.

The very word they shout, "Hosanna!" is a Hebrew expression meaning "Save!" This word embodies the very meaning of the name "Jesus."

PRAYER: Lord, how I need deliverance from my sins and circumstances! Sometimes I'm too proud to admit my need, but reality drives me to my knees. Your name is both a prayer and the answer to my prayer. Thank you for saving me. Amen.

EPISODE 66

A LESSON FROM THE FIG TREE

11:11 Jesus entered Jerusalem and went to the temple. He looked around at everything, but since it was already late, he went out to Bethany with the Twelve.

Jesus takes stock of the situation, then decides to spend the night in a nearby village, probably at the home of his friends Mary, Martha, and Lazarus.

12 The next day as they were leaving Bethany, Jesus was hungry. 13 Seeing in the distance a fig tree in leaf, he went to find out if it had any fruit. When he reached it, he found nothing but leaves, because it was not the season for figs. 14 Then he said to the tree, "May no one ever eat fruit from you again." And his disciples heard him say it.

Admittedly, this is an odd event. Mark emphasizes there are several witnesses to this peculiar event. It's as if he's writing, "I didn't make this up...really!"

Jesus shouldn't be surprised—much less angry—that this fig tree isn't bearing fruit out of season. But Christ's judgment isn't just about the tree; it's also about a nation.

The fig tree symbolizes Israel, who will soon reject and crucify God's Son. Even though Israel will always be the "apple of God's eye," the Lord will nonetheless judge and discipline his rebellious people as part of his redemptive plan. This generation will see the utter destruction of Jerusalem and the desecration of its Temple.

PRAYER: Father in Heaven, your justice calls us to repentance. Our rebellion will not go unpunished forever. Help me humble myself, pray, seek your face, and turn from my ways so that you will forgive and restore me. Amen.

EPISODE 67

WRECKING THE
MONEY CHANGERS

11:15 On reaching Jerusalem, Jesus entered the temple area and began driving out those who were buying and selling there. He overturned the tables of the money changers and the benches of those selling doves, 16 and would not allow anyone to carry merchandise through the temple courts.

A bustling marketplace has grown up around God's holy Temple. Profiteers hawk ceremonially clean animals to the religious pilgrims who have come to offer a sacrifice. Worshipers are also told they need to purchase ceremonially clean money if they want their offerings to be accepted by God. The Son of God is righteously angered by the exploitation of those who have come to worship his Father.

To add insult to injury, vendors are using the temple courts as a shortcut through the city, clogging the sacred walkways with merchandise and traffic. For Jesus, this is just too much.

17 And as he taught them, he said, "Is it not written: "'My house will be called a house of prayer for all nations'? But you have made it 'a den of robbers.'" 18 The chief priests and the teachers of the law heard this and began looking for a way to kill him, for they feared him, because the whole crowd was amazed at his teaching.19 When evening came, Jesus and his disciples went out of the city.

Normally, those who witness someone wrecking the booths at an outdoor market would call for the authorities. But in this situation, the crowd is awestruck by Christ's teaching and testimony. Everyone, of course, except the chief priests and teachers of the law, who are more determined than ever to kill him.

PRAYER: Jesus, overturn the tables in my life. Upset my complacency. Disrupt my expediency. Give me your godly anger when others are exploited in the name of religion or commerce. Make your church a house of prayer for all people. Amen.

EPISODE 68

ANOTHER LESSON FROM
THE FIG TREE

*11:20 In the morning, as they went along, they saw
the fig tree withered from the roots. 21 Peter
remembered and said to Jesus, "Rabbi, look! The fig
tree you cursed has withered!" 22 "Have faith in
God," Jesus answered. 23 "Truly I tell you, if anyone
says to this mountain, 'Go, throw yourself into the
sea,' and does not doubt in their heart but believes that
what they say will happen, it will be done for them.*

Faith in God is a powerful thing.
But it's not about seeing who can rub the genie's
lamp the hardest. Nor is it about using God to get
what we want or explaining away that which we don't
understand.

No. Faith means trusting both the heart and the
hand of God to transform our hearts and move our
hands. It's being "all in," even when things don't
immediately turn out the way we expect.

Faith means making my will, Thy will.

Once that happens, there is nothing beyond our
grasp because it's God who is doing the reaching.

Jesus tells his disciples that we shouldn't be

surprised when our belief in God produces tangible results. Withering a fig tree or laying waste the powers of hell—they're one in the same for the believer who calls upon the Lord and expects him to answer.

> *24 Therefore I tell you, whatever you ask for in prayer, believe that you have received it, and it will be yours. 25 And when you stand praying, if you hold anything against anyone, forgive them, so that your Father in heaven may forgive you your sins."*

Jesus tells the crowd that effective prayer has upward, inward and outward dimensions.

Our requests must first be in sync with God's purpose. Then, our hearts must conceive that which our eyes don't see. Finally, if our fists are clinched in anger against others, then our palms can't be open to receive what God wants to give us. Forgiveness is the key.

I can't tell you why God seems to answer some prayers and not others. I can only tell you that talking with God is a good thing and that forgiving others is a good thing. And that being forgiven is a great thing.

If the Lord uses my need to help me become more dependent upon him, then so be it. Or if God chooses to meet the need that has brought me to deeper dependence, then so much the better.

Jesus is telling his friends that, in his kingdom, true faith can move the Father's heart. And if faith can move heaven, then moving the earth will be easy.

PRAYER: Father, let my will become thy will. Help me trust you to move the mountains in my life and in the lives of those I love—those whom you love infinitely more. Amen.

EPISODE 69

BY WHOSE AUTHORITY?

11:27 They arrived again in Jerusalem, and while Jesus was walking in the temple courts, the chief priests, the teachers of the law and the elders came to him. 28 "By what authority are you doing these things?" they asked. "And who gave you authority to do this?"

These Jewish leaders ask the same central question that Mark answers throughout his gospel: "Just who are you, Jesus?"

Of course they know he's Mary's son, the carpenter from Galilee. They know he's a rabbi with a band of fervent disciples who attracts thousands with his teaching and preaching. They've heard he shows compassion to the poor and disenfranchised. And he seems to be able to heal the sick and release people from spiritual bondage. All this seems good.

But Jesus breaks the Sabbath, rejects strict religious traditions, and criticizes the rich and self-sufficient. More worrisome, he calls himself "The Son of Man," an Old Testament reference to the Jewish Messiah who will deliver Israel. And most distressing, he seems to claim that he's the Son of God, a claim they consider to be the ultimate blasphemy.

When the religious leaders demand Jesus tell them who has authorized his actions, they fully expect him to declare himself as God's Son. This will allow them to arrest Jesus for blasphemy and accuse him of sedition. But Jesus won't allow these men to dictate the time and circumstances of his sacrifice; so he responds with a riddle:

> *29 Jesus replied, "I will ask you one question. Answer me, and I will tell you by what authority I am doing these things. 30 John's baptism—was it from heaven, or of human origin? Tell me!" 31 They discussed it among themselves and said, "If we say, 'From heaven,' he will ask, 'Then why didn't you believe him?' 32 But if we say, 'Of human origin'...." (They feared the people, for everyone held that John really was a prophet.) 33 So they answered Jesus, "We don't know." Jesus said, "Neither will I tell you by what authority I am doing these things."*

The claims of Jesus collide with our preconceptions, prejudices, and desires.

The elders and priests have a power base to protect. The people of Israel have an oppressor to oust. The sick and needy have problems of their own.

Everyone has an agenda. We're all looking for a messiah who will fit into our plans, meet our needs, and solve our problems.

But what if Jesus' plan is so much bigger than simply filling in the missing pieces in our personal puzzles? What if he invaded our story to invite us into his? What if—instead of trying to get Jesus to acquiesce to our authority—the secret is to submit ourselves to his?

PRAYER: Jesus, unmask my true agenda. Wreck my small thinking and meager faith. Reveal your true self so that I might both repent and rejoice before you—for you are so much more than I've ever imagined. Amen.

MARK 12

EPISODE 70

AN OUTRAGEOUS CONSPIRACY

In a matter of days, Jesus will be hanging on an executioner's cross on a hill outside the capital city of Israel. His time is short, so every word must count.

> *12:1 Jesus then began to speak to them in parables: "A man planted a vineyard. He put a wall around it, dug a pit for the winepress and built a watchtower. Then he rented the vineyard to some farmers and moved to another place. 2 At harvest time he sent a servant to the tenants to collect from them some of the fruit of the vineyard."*

Up to this point, the tale is benign—if not idyllic. But it's about to take a nasty turn.

> *3 "But they seized him, beat him and sent him away empty-handed. 4 Then he sent another servant to them; they struck this man on the head and treated him shamefully. 5 He sent still another, and that one*

they killed. He sent many others; some of them they beat, others they killed. 6 He had one left to send, a son, whom he loved. He sent him last of all, saying, 'They will respect my son.' 7 But the tenants said to one another, 'This is the heir. Come, let's kill him, and the inheritance will be ours.' 8 So they took him and killed him, and threw him out of the vineyard."

Jesus provokes the righteous indignation of the crowd. This kind of behavior is outrageous and appalling! Where is justice?

9 "What then will the owner of the vineyard do? He will come and kill those tenants and give the vineyard to others. 10 Haven't you read this scripture: " 'The stone the builders rejected has become the cornerstone; 11 the Lord has done this, and it is marvelous in our eyes'?"

When Christ quotes a psalm of King David—a prophecy about the coming Messiah—the crowd realizes that this parable isn't about some rebellious tenants. Rather, Jesus is calling down condemnation on those who have rejected Israel's prophets and who are on the verge of putting God's Son to death.

12 Then the chief priests, the teachers of the law and the elders looked for a way to arrest him because they knew he had spoken the parable against them. But they were afraid of the crowd; so they left him and went away. 13 Later they sent some of the Pharisees and Herodians to Jesus to catch him in his words.

The politicians and the priests—often bitter enemies—now conspire to accuse and convict Jesus of whatever charge they can fabricate.

PRAYER: Jesus, the proud and powerful rejected you then, and they refuse you today. And yet, a final reckoning will not be denied or delayed by the efforts of men. You are faultless, your judgments are true, and your return is certain. Amen.

EPISODE 71

HONORING THE IMAGE

The cat and mouse game continues. The Herodians are the political supporters of Herod, the regional governor. Ordinarily, they observe an uneasy truce with the Jewish religious leaders. But both groups are now allied against Jesus, whom they fear will incite a rebellion against Rome. So the Herodians approach Jesus, imagining they can pander to his sense of Jewish nationalism, hoping to trap him into committing treason against Caesar.

> *12:14 They came to him and said, "Teacher, we know you are a man of integrity. You aren't swayed by others, because you pay no attention to who they are; but you teach the way of God in accordance with the truth. Is it right to pay the imperial tax to Caesar or not?*

The Jews are a fiercely proud people and paying tribute to their Roman oppressors is offensive and degrading. But to ignore the imperial tax is to invite punishment—or worse.

15 Should we pay or shouldn't we?" But Jesus knew their hypocrisy. "Why are you trying to trap me?" he asked. "Bring me a denarius and let me look at it." 16 They brought the coin, and he asked them, "Whose image is this? And whose inscription?" "Caesar's," they replied. 17 Then Jesus said to them, "Give to Caesar what is Caesar's and to God what is God's." And they were amazed at him.

Again, Jesus will not be trapped into supplying them with the evidence they need to arrest him. But he also uses this opportunity to illustrate a kingdom principle: we can comfortably surrender to earthly authorities that which bears its mark, for the things of this world will eventually pass away. More importantly, we should give to God that which bears his image: namely, ourselves. In doing so, we lay up in heaven that which is truly valuable and ultimately eternal.

PRAYER: Lord, help me recognize and value your image in me and in those around me. Let me invest myself in that which brings you eternal glory rather than in what will pass away. For you are Lord of heaven and earth. Amen.

EPISODE 72

MARRIAGE AT THE RESURRECTION?

12:18 Then the Sadducees, who say there is no resurrection, came to him with a question.

The Sadducees are a rival religious sect who compete with the Pharisees for power and popularity among the Jews. Not only do the Sadducees want to discredit Jesus, they also want to refute the whole idea of eternal life—one of Christ's central teachings.

19 "Teacher," they said, "Moses wrote for us that if a man's brother dies and leaves a wife but no children, the man must marry the widow and raise up offspring for his brother. 20 Now there were seven brothers. The first one married and died without leaving any children. 21 The second one married the widow, but he also died, leaving no child. It was the same with the third. 22 In fact, none of the seven left any children. Last of all, the woman died too. 23 At the resurrection whose wife will she be, since the seven were married to her?"

The Sadducees hold a faith without hope. Although they ostensibly believe in an eternal God, they refuse to believe he created mankind to live for eternity. Like many people today, they practice a futile faith. Confident in their skepticism, they challenge Jesus with a question they think will disprove the possibility of eternal life.

> *24 Jesus replied, "Are you not in error because you do not know the Scriptures or the power of God? 25 When the dead rise, they will neither marry nor be given in marriage; they will be like the angels in heaven. 26 Now about the dead rising—have you not read in the book of Moses, in the account of the burning bush, how God said to him, 'I am the God of Abraham, the God of Isaac, and the God of Jacob'? 27 He is not the God of the dead, but of the living. You are badly mistaken!"*

Jesus wastes no words in pointing out their error.

Although the Sadducees consider themselves religious authorities, they don't allow God's Word to govern their lives. Rather, they bend Scripture to accommodate their own agenda and worldview. People who do this divorce themselves from the Bible's truth and power. If the Sadducees really knew the truth and power of God's Word, they would have already seen that God describes himself as Lord of the eternally living.

Because of this, the Sadducees fundamentally misunderstand the nature of eternal life. They suppose that the afterlife—*if it exists*—is simply an extension of this earthly existence. How boring!

Jesus pulls back the veil and reveals that those who rise again to eternal life will have glorious, supernatural bodies. We will have no need of marriage or family because the closeness we share with God and one another will surpass any intimacy we experience in our mortality.

Only a person from a foreign country can speak authoritatively of his homeland. Jesus came from heaven; so no one knows more about its reality than he does.

PRAYER: Jesus, although many have gone to heaven, you are the One who has come from there. You reveal the truth because you are the Truth. Not only do I want to know the Scriptures, I want to know their Author. Teach me your Word and give me your power—not so that I might be right, but rather so that you might be glorified. Amen.

EPISODE 73

THE GREATEST COMMANDMENT

Christ has been challenged by the pious and then by the skeptics. Now, the lawyers will take their turn.

> *12:28 One of the teachers of the law came and heard them debating. Noticing that Jesus had given them a good answer, he asked him, "Of all the commandments, which is the most important?"*

To the Jew, the Law embodies God's plan, purpose, and promises for humanity. As soon as they can speak, Hebrew children begin memorizing Scripture. Religious men wear small leather boxes containing verses on their arms and heads called "phylacteries" as reminders of God's commands. They even carve scriptures on the doorposts of their homes. The Law is everything.

So when an expert in the Torah asks Jesus to sum up the whole Law, it's a profound and potentially daunting question. But Jesus has an advantage: he knows the Law's Author. His Father is Creation's Judge. Christ himself is the Wonderful Counselor. So his response isn't just theological, it's personal.

29 "The most important one," answered Jesus, "is this: 'Hear, O Israel, The Lord our God, the Lord is one. 30 Love the Lord your God with all your heart and with all your soul and with all your mind and with all your strength.' 31 The second is this: 'Love your neighbor as yourself.' There is no commandment greater than these."

Christ reaffirms the truth revealed by God to Moses in the Pentateuch, the first five books of Jewish law and history: the sovereign God of the universe is without rival or comparison. As such, he demands and deserves our wholehearted adoration and obedience. But this vertical devotion has a horizontal dimension: our love for God is in vain without compassion to those around us.

These commands not only sum up the core of the Old Testament but the heart of the New Testament as well.

32 "Well said, teacher," the man replied. "You are right in saying that God is one and there is no other but him. 33 To love him with all your heart, with all your understanding and with all your strength, and to love your neighbor as yourself is more important than all burnt offerings and sacrifices." 34 When Jesus saw that he had answered wisely, he said to him, "You are not far from the kingdom of God." And from then on no one dared ask him any more questions.

[Jesus says that a lawyer is on the verge of God's Kingdom? Could this be one of the Bible's little-known miracles?]

When Jesus visited Jerusalem as a boy, his parents unintentionally left him behind in the Temple as their family entourage made its way home to Nazareth. When they discovered he was missing, they returned to find him in the Temple courts, amazing the experts and teachers in the law with his spiritual insight. Now, at the end of his ministry, Jesus returns to "his Father's house" and once again astounds Jewish leaders and laypersons with the depth of his understanding.

PRAYER: Lord, it's not enough for me just to write your Law on my doorpost and wear it on my forehead. Rather, I pray that you'll inscribe your Word on my heart so that my life will overflow with your justice, truth, and mercy. Amen.

EPISODE 74

WHOSE SON IS THE MESSIAH?

12:35 While Jesus was teaching in the temple courts, he asked, "Why do the teachers of the law say that the Messiah is the son of David? 36 David himself, speaking by the Holy Spirit, declared: "'The Lord said to my Lord: 'Sit at my right hand until I put your enemies under your feet.' 37 David himself calls him 'Lord.' How then can he be his son?" The large crowd listened to him with delight.

Biblical prophecy is often best understood looking backward rather than forward. Prophecies prove God's immutable plans as much as they reveal them. They show us that the Lord can be trusted because he has designed and destined the details of our redemption. Although we may look forward "as through a glass darkly," we can look back with exhilarating clarity.

The Jewish Scriptures contain many specific prophecies about the coming Messiah. Some foretell his First Advent: incarnation, birth, suffering, death, and resurrection. Other prophecies refer to his Second Advent: glorious return, defeat of heaven's enemies, final judgment, and restoration of all things. Without the insight of the Holy Spirit, it's confusing for even the most studied scholar to discern which prophecies apply when.

In Jesus' day, some religious teachers held that the Messiah would be a descendant of King David, while others argued that David would not have called his own son "Lord."

This is the question that Jesus addresses while teaching in the Temple courts. Because he is both the Son of God and a son of David, Jesus himself is the answer to this scriptural riddle.

David was the greatest king in Jewish history. He defeated Israel's enemies, made preparations for the construction of the Temple, and composed the lion's share of the Psalms. And yet, Jesus declares that King David foresaw that his Lord, God, would esteem another Lord, the Messiah, as even greater than himself.

Jesus' family line leads directly back to King David. In fact, Christ was born in "David's City," Bethlehem, because King Herod had commanded that every family return to their ancestral homes for the national census. Jesus, a son of David, fulfills King David's prophecy that his descendant, the Messiah, will share the heavenly throne with God himself.

As the time for Jesus' sacrifice approaches, he unequivocally proclaims that he's not only the fulfillment of the prophets, but of the whole Law itself.

PRAYER: Lord, you keep every promise you make. Help me trust your plan and purpose for my life and the world, even when it's hard for me to understand. I am confident that one day I'll look back and see how all the pieces fit in place. In the meantime, I will delight in you and your Word. Amen.

EPISODE 75

RELIGIOUS HYPOCRITES
AND PREDATORS

12:38 As he taught, Jesus said, "Watch out for the teachers of the law. They like to walk around in flowing robes and be greeted with respect in the marketplaces, 39 and have the most important seats in the synagogues and the places of honor at banquets. 40 They devour widows' houses and for a show make lengthy prayers. Such men will be punished most severely."

Jesus is angry because these religious hypocrites not only misrepresent his Father's character, but they also oppress the very ones they're called to love and serve.

It's remarkable that Jesus seems to have infinite compassion for sinners but no tolerance at all for the self-righteous. Pride and privilege have no place in his kingdom.

Jesus proclaims that people who use religion for their own selfish purposes will face severe punishment from God. He warns us to watch out for them, and in doing so, he implicitly warns us to keep ourselves from this kind of predatory behavior.

PRAYER: Lord, give me discernment about those I trust spiritually. Likewise, deliver me from my own arrogance, entitlement, and hypocrisy. Help me serve and honor you and others before myself. Amen.

EPISODE 76

WHOSE GIFT IS GREATER?

12:41 Jesus sat down opposite the place where the offerings were put and watched the crowd putting their money into the temple treasury. Many rich people threw in large amounts. 42 But a poor widow came and put in two very small copper coins, worth only a few cents. 43 Calling his disciples to him, Jesus said, "Truly I tell you, this poor widow has put more into the treasury than all the others. 44 They all gave out of their wealth; but she, out of her poverty, put in everything—all she had to live on."

As Jesus teaches in the Temple courts, he watches the religious elite flaunt their power and position. He sees the rich make pious displays of their public giving. Christ wants us to know that his kingdom looks nothing like this. In fact, one day, this upside down world will be righted as the first become last and the meek inherit the earth.

In the meantime, Christ reveals a powerful truth about giving: it's not the amount of our gift that matters; rather, it's the condition of our hearts.

The Lord knows how easy it is for us to be

defined by what we have and what we want. Unless we practice giving our stuff away, our stuff will own us. And until we learn to give sacrificially, the power of mammon in our lives will not be tamed.

God doesn't want our money; he wants us.

He doesn't want our time; he wants us.

And until he's Lord of our money and time, he isn't really our Lord at all.

PRAYER: Heavenly Father, help me acknowledge you as the creator and owner of everything. I am your steward, entrusted to use everything for your glory, others' blessing, and my provision. In light of your grace and love to me, let me live a life of boundless gratitude and extravagant generosity. Amen.

MARK 13

EPISODE 77

SIGNS OF THE END OF THIS AGE

It's one thing to preach selflessness and to care for the sick, but it's quite another to predict the end of the world.

Jesus, however, isn't a moralist; he's the Messiah.

He wants us to understand that history is relentlessly heading toward the establishment of God's kingdom. But before this new world is resurrected, the old one will meet with utter devastation and God's people will face unparalleled persecution.

> *13:1 As Jesus was leaving the temple, one of his disciples said to him, "Look, Teacher! What massive stones! What magnificent buildings!" 2 "Do you see all these great buildings?" replied Jesus. "Not one stone here will be left on another; every one will be thrown down."*

The Jews had a simple test for any prophet: if their predictions came true, then the messenger was from God. If not, then their words were to be disregarded.

In 70 AD, almost three decades after Jesus'

prophecy, the Roman Emperor Titus and his army destroyed Jerusalem and its Temple. The Jewish readers of Mark's Gospel would have recognized that Jesus' claims were true, since his prophecy about the destruction of the Temple was fulfilled in clear detail.

Jesus and his followers leave the heart of Jerusalem and walk a short way to the ridge of hills just east of the city.

> *3 As Jesus was sitting on the Mount of Olives opposite the temple, Peter, James, John and Andrew asked him privately, 4 "Tell us, when will these things happen? And what will be the sign that they are all about to be fulfilled?"*

The disciples assume that the imminent destruction of the Temple and the establishment of God's kingdom on earth will coincide. But this isn't the case.

Jesus knows what he will suffer in the coming days and what his followers will face in the coming years. He also knows what his church must endure in the centuries to come. So he sits down with his inner circle and prepares them for the tribulations ahead.

He tells them they will face spiritual deception, yet they don't have to be deceived. They will face worldwide chaos and destruction, yet they don't have to be fearful. They will even face persecution and death, yet they don't have to despair. When these things happen, they can take heart because history is unfolding just as Christ said it would.

Jesus reveals a dozen key signs that will precede his return at the end of this age:

- Counterfeit spirituality:

  5 Jesus said to them: "Watch out that no one deceives you. 6 Many will come in my name, claiming, 'I am he,' and will deceive many.

- International wars:

  7 When you hear of wars and rumors of wars, do not be alarmed. Such things must happen, but the end is still to come. 8 Nation will rise against nation, and kingdom against kingdom.

- Natural disasters:

  There will be earthquakes in various places, and famines. These are the beginning of birth pains.

- Tremendous persecution:

  9 You must be on your guard. You will be handed over to the local councils and flogged in the synagogues. On account of me you will stand before governors and kings as witnesses to them.

- Worldwide evangelism:

  10 And the gospel must first be preached to all nations. 11 Whenever you are arrested and brought to trial, do not worry beforehand about what to say. Just say whatever is given you at the time, for it is not you speaking, but the Holy Spirit.

- Family betrayal:

  12 Brother will betray brother to death, and a father his child. Children will rebel against their parents and have them put to death.13 Everyone will hate you because of me, but the one who stands firm to the end will be saved.

- The Antichrist in the Temple:

  14 When you see 'the abomination that causes desolation' standing where it does not belong—let the reader understand—then let those who are in Judea flee to the mountains.

- Panic in Israel:

  15 Let no one on the roof of his house go down or enter the house to take anything out. 16 Let no one in the field go back to get his cloak. 17 How dreadful it will be in those days for pregnant women and nursing mothers!

- Unprecedented suffering:

  18 Pray that this will not take place in winter, 19 because those will be days of distress unequaled from the beginning, when God created the world, until now—and never to be equaled again. 20 If the Lord had not cut short those days, no one would survive. But for the sake of the elect, whom he has chosen, he has shortened them.

- False messiahs:

  21 At that time if anyone says to you, 'Look, here is the Messiah!' or, 'Look, there he is!' do not believe it. 22 For false messiahs and false prophets will appear and perform signs and wonders to deceive, if possible, even the elect.

- Signs in the heavens:

  23 So be on your guard; I have told you everything ahead of time. 24 "But in those days, following that distress, 'the sun will be darkened, and the moon will not give its light; 25 the stars will fall from the sky, and the heavenly bodies will be shaken.'

- The return of Christ for his followers:

  26 At that time men will see the Son of Man coming in clouds with great power and glory. 27 And he will send his angels and gather his elect from the four winds, from the ends of the earth to the ends of the heavens. 28 "Now learn this lesson from the fig tree: As soon as its twigs get tender and its leaves come out, you know that summer is near. 29 Even so, when you see these things happening, you know that it is near, right at the door."

As God's Son, Jesus is privy to his Father's plan for the redemption of our fallen world. As our Savior, Jesus shares some of that knowledge with us so that we won't be undone by what we will face. Rather, we'll see God's hand at work in even the most dire of world events, and take comfort and strength from the fact that all of history is moving inevitably toward Christ's triumph over evil and the establishment of God's Kingdom.

PRAYER: Lord, rather than being overwhelmed by the chaos and carnage in the world, help me overcome by my confidence in you and your coming kingdom. I can put my hope in you because you died and rose again to make all things new. Amen.

EPISODE 78

BE VIGILANT AND FAITHFUL

13:30 I tell you the truth, this generation will certainly not pass away until all these things have happened. 31 Heaven and earth will pass away, but my words will never pass away.

Jesus tells all those who will listen that his words are just as immutable and reliable as his Father's. He states that God's children—the generation who have been adopted by grace through faith—will see his every promise and prediction fulfilled.

32 "But about that day or hour no one knows, not even the angels in heaven, nor the Son, but only the Father. 33 Be on guard! Be alert! You do not know when that time will come. 34 It's like a man going away: He leaves his house and puts his servants in charge, each with his assigned task, and tells the one at the door to keep watch. 35 "Therefore keep watch because you do not know when the owner of the house will come back—whether in the evening, or at midnight, or when the rooster crows, or at dawn. 36 If he comes suddenly, do not let him find you sleeping. 37

What I say to you, I say to everyone: 'Watch!' "

Jesus' message is clear: *Be vigilant! Be prayerful! Be confident!*

Jesus calls his followers to live with a sense of impending glory. To rise every morning knowing that...

...we are one day nearer to the consummation of our heart's deepest desires.

...the world's agonizing labor pains will soon give way to the birth of a new heaven and new earth.

...nothing enters our lives that does not first pass through God's hands.

...time is not our enemy and circumstances are not our foe.

...Jesus endured the Cross so that we, too, will be victorious over what is before us.

PRAYER: Jesus, empower me by your Holy Spirit to burn more brightly as the world darkens and to be more loving as the world becomes more evil. Help me live with sober intentionality and joyful expectancy. Even so, Lord Jesus, quickly come! Amen.

MARK 14

EPISODE 79

BROKEN AND POURED OUT

The festival of Passover, along with the holy days of Pentecost and Tabernacles, was observed by every Jew who could make the pilgrimage to the Temple in Jerusalem. Jesus and the Twelve were there, along with Jews from every part of Israel and the surrounding lands.

> *14:1 Now the Passover and the Feast of Unleavened Bread were only two days away, and the chief priests and the teachers of the law were scheming for some way to arrest Jesus secretly and kill him. 2 "But not during the Feast," they said, "or the people may riot."*

The Festival of Unleavened Bread was a weeklong commemoration that culminated with the one-day celebration of the Passover. According to Scripture, the Hebrew exodus from Egypt was so abrupt that they didn't even have time for their bread to properly rise in their ovens. Hence, the Jews celebrated their sudden and miraculous deliverance from slavery by eating flat, unleavened bread called matzo.

3 While he was in Bethany, reclining at the table in the home of Simon the Leper, a woman came with an alabaster jar of very expensive perfume, made of pure nard. She broke the jar and poured the perfume on his head. 4 Some of those present were saying indignantly to one another, "Why this waste of perfume? 5 It could have been sold for more than a year's wages and the money given to the poor." And they rebuked her harshly. 6 "Leave her alone," said Jesus. "Why are you bothering her? She has done a beautiful thing to me. 7 The poor you will always have with you, and you can help them any time you want. But you will not always have me. 8 She did what she could. She poured perfume on my body beforehand to prepare for my burial. 9 Truly I tell you, wherever the gospel is preached throughout the world, what she has done will also be told, in memory of her."

This event explodes with meaning.

First, the setting is the home of a man known as Simon the Leper. The very fact that a crowd of Jews could be celebrating the Passover in the home of a man who was once "unclean" is miraculous.

Into this improbable scene comes an even more unlikely act: a woman breaks open an ornamental jar of expensive perfume and begins pouring it on Jesus' head. The nard is worth more than a year's wages—a veritable fortune in a day where most people live hand to mouth.

John's Gospel identifies the woman as Mary of Bethany. Jesus was a familiar guest in the house she shared with her sister, Martha, and their brother,

Lazarus. This public "anointing" near the end of Jesus' earthly mission harkens back to his public baptism at the beginning of his ministry three years earlier. It also reminds those closest to Christ of the precious burial balms of frankincense and myrrh brought by the magi at his birth.

Most importantly, Jesus says that this act foreshadows the coming events of the week when his lifeless body will be anointed for burial, wrapped in grave cloths, and sealed in a stone tomb.

While the Son of God is clearly moved by Mary's extravagance, some of those around him are visibly offended.

What kind of woman would dare to touch a prophet, much less pour priceless perfume on him? Such a patently wasteful and offensive act! And how could a true man of God allow such a treasure to be squandered instead of sold and the proceeds used to help the needy?

Jesus' response offends the offended: "*If you truly want to serve the poor, you'll always have plenty of opportunity. But the chance to lavish me with love is quickly slipping away.*"

Honoring Christ does not preclude our caring for the poor any more than caring for the poor precludes our worship of Christ. It's not *either/or,* it's *both/and* since it is God's provision that ultimately allows for both. But for Judas, the world is full of limitations. As treasurer of the Twelve, he cannot embezzle funds he never receives. Jesus' celebration of Mary's extravagance is the final straw.

PRAYER: Jesus, this woman took her most precious possession and poured it out in love to you. This is what your Father has done by allowing his beloved Son to be broken and poured out on my behalf. Love so amazing, so divine, demands my soul, my life, my all. Amen.

EPISODE 80

SOLD OUT BY A CONFIDANT

14:10 Then Judas Iscariot, one of the Twelve, went to the chief priests to betray Jesus to them. 11 They were delighted to hear this and promised to give him money. So he watched for an opportunity to hand him over.

Time after time, Israel's religious leaders have tried to ensnare and arrest Jesus. Their efforts have been thwarted until now. Friend and foe scheme to compel Christ to the cross.

And yet, this is no mere lynching.

It happens solely because Father and Son have conspired to redeem the very people who will nail Jesus to the tree.

His time is at hand.

PRAYER: Father, before we sinned, you planned our redemption. You even used Christ's betrayal as a means to our salvation. Thank you for sending your Son that I might know your mercy and grace. Amen.

EPISODE 81

BEHIND THE SCENES

14:12 On the first day of the Feast of Unleavened Bread, when it was customary to sacrifice the Passover lamb, Jesus' disciples asked him, "Where do you want us to go and make preparations for you to eat the Passover?" 13 So he sent two of his disciples, telling them, "Go into the city, and a man carrying a jar of water will meet you. Follow him. 14 Say to the owner of the house he enters, 'The Teacher asks: Where is my guest room, where I may eat the Passover with my disciples?' 15 He will show you a large room upstairs, furnished and ready. Make preparations for us there." 16 The disciples left, went into the city and found things just as Jesus had told them. So they prepared the Passover.

The time has come for Jesus' last meal with his closest followers. He chooses the occasion of the Passover celebration, marking God's deliverance of the Hebrews from Egypt's cruel hand.

Before humanity was even aware of its need, the Omnipotent Father had purposed to meet it through the sacrifice of his Son. Likewise, even in the smallest details of preparing a room for a religious meal, the Sovereign God was working behind the scenes to accomplish his plan.

Were these two disciples accustomed to the fact that everything was just as Jesus had told them it would be? Or did they continue to be amazed at his lordship over circumstances and at their own lack of faith?

PRAYER: Lord, forgive me when I "sweat the details." Instead, let me hear and obey you so that I might find things just as you said they would be. Help me recognize your gracious and mighty hand in the smallest of details and in the most worrisome of circumstances. I will trust you. Amen.

EPISODE 82

TRAITOR AT THE TABLE

14:17 When evening came, Jesus arrived with the Twelve. 18 While they were reclining at the table eating, he said, "I tell you the truth, one of you will betray me—one who is eating with me." 19 They were saddened, and one by one they said to him, "Surely you don't mean me?" 20 "It is one of the Twelve," he replied, "one who dips bread into the bowl with me. 21 The Son of Man will go just as it is written about him. But woe to that man who betrays the Son of Man! It would be better for him if he had not been born."

God is never surprised by sin. In fact, Jesus makes it a point to let everyone around the table know that he's fully aware of what's in their hearts. In conveying his foreknowledge, Jesus demonstrates his divinity and lordship over every circumstance, no matter how evil.

Does Judas choose to betray Christ?

Apparently.

Is it inevitable that he does this?

Apparently.

How can these two things be reconciled?

I don't know.

For centuries, theologians, philosophers, and even scientists have debated the issues of foreknowledge, predestination, free will, and the sovereignty of God.

While I believe we should continue pressing toward a fuller understanding of these issues, my trust in God doesn't depend on my comprehension of how everything works.

To do so would be like my refusing to get into a fully loaded passenger jet until I fully understood how something weighing nearly 900,000 pounds can lift into the sky and fly at nearly the speed of sound. I am comfortable admitting that I don't understand everything while relying upon the knowledge and good will of those who do.

It's not a perfect metaphor, but it demonstrates how trust can function in the absence of total understanding.

The Messiah's betrayal is clearly foretold by Scripture. The betrayer's identity is clearly foreknown by Jesus. And yet, each man lives and dies by the choices he makes.

PRAYER: Lord of Heaven and Earth, help me live with the ever-present peace of your sovereignty guarding my heart from fear and anxiety. Likewise, let me measure my motives and choices, knowing that my decisions matter. Most importantly, let me rejoice in the fact that you invite deniers and betrayers to your table so that we all might be saved. Amen.

EPISODE 83

HIS BODY AND BLOOD

14:22 While they were eating, Jesus took bread, and when he had given thanks, he broke it and gave it to his disciples, saying, "Take it; this is my body." 23 Then he took a cup, and when he had given thanks, he gave it to them, and they all drank from it. 24 "This is my blood of the [new] covenant, which is poured out for many," he said to them. 25 "I tell you, I will not drink again of the fruit of the vine until that day when I drink it new in the kingdom of God." 26 When they had sung a hymn, they went out to the Mount of Olives.

While it may be tempting to think that Jesus appropriates the imagery of the Passover meal for his own message, the Last Supper is actually the fullest expression of the realities that are merely prefigured in the Passover.

Throughout the Old Testament, God Almighty set the terms of his relationship with humanity through an emerging series of covenants made with Adam, Noah, Abraham, and Moses, among others. Judaism evolved as the observance of these covenant rules and rituals.

But Jesus isn't just offering the world the next level in the evolution of Judaism. Rather, Christ is fulfilling the Law and the Prophets. He says that his body is the bread symbolized by the unleavened matzo and his blood is the life poured out by the slain Passover lamb. Everything that came before points to him because his sacrifice is the new, final, complete, and ultimate covenant of God's provision for man's sinfulness.

Jesus is so sure of this truth that he seals his promise with a toast, a solemn vow: I will not drink wine again until my mission is accomplished and my kingdom is inaugurated.

PRAYER: Jesus, we're awed that you not only invite us to your table, but you've become our life-giving, death-defying, heart-transforming feast. So we examine ourselves, confessing our unworthiness and repenting of the things in our life that called you to the cross. We take your body and blood so that judgment may pass over us and so that we might be sealed for life everlasting. We remember your love and proclaim your lordship until we come home to you or you come home to us. Amen.

EPISODE 84

DESERTION AND DENIAL

W hat are his friends thinking? Has Jesus finally crossed the line by comparing his body and blood with the sacred Passover meal?

> *14:27 "You will all fall away," Jesus told them, "for it is written: 'I will strike the shepherd, and the sheep will be scattered.' 28 But after I have risen, I will go ahead of you into Galilee."*

As they leave the Upper Room and walk back toward the garden at the foot of the Mount of Olives, Christ reveals that--although one disciple will betray him—every one of them will desert him. He quotes a passage from Zechariah that predicts the Messiah will be struck down and his flock scattered. But Jesus follows this troubling revelation with his promise to rise from the dead and rejoin them in Galilee.

> *29 Peter declared, "Even if all fall away, I will not." 30 "Truly I tell you," Jesus answered, "today—yes, tonight—before the rooster crows twice you yourself will disown me three times." 31 But Peter insisted emphatically, "Even if I have to die with you, I will never disown you." And all the others said the same.*

Perhaps Jesus had tears in his eyes as he quietly told his closest friends what lay before them all: betrayal, denial, inquisition, and death. Perhaps he smiled sadly at the Twelve's insistence that they would die before ever disowning him. No doubt they were earnest, but their resolve would be undone by forces greater than their best intentions.

PRAYER: Lord, I confess that I can't live up to my own expectations—much less yours. It's only by your sacrifice and your Spirit that I can become like you. Thank you for keeping your promises even when I can't keep mine. Fill me with your power so that I might love well, live well, and bring you glory. Amen.

EPISODE 85

OVERWHELMED AT
GETHSEMANE

*14:32 They went to a place called Gethsemane, and
Jesus said to his disciples, "Sit here while I pray." 33
He took Peter, James and John along with him, and
he began to be deeply distressed and troubled. 34 "My
soul is overwhelmed with sorrow to the point of death,"
he said to them. "Stay here and keep watch." 35
Going a little farther, he fell to the ground and prayed
that if possible the hour might pass from him. 36
"Abba, Father," he said, "everything is possible for
you. Take this cup from me. Yet not what I will, but
what you will."*

Though Christ is understandably distraught by the
knowledge of his imminent torture and execution,
he's even more overwhelmed by the prospect of
bearing the punishment for the sins of every man,
woman and child who will ever live. That price—
worse than the unbearable physical pain—will be the
loss of the relationship he's enjoyed with his Father
from before the beginning of time. For the first time
ever, he'll be absolutely alone, executed by the very

men whose condemnation he'll bear to hell and back. Facing this crisis, Jesus does the same thing he's done every day of his ministry: he prays. He cries "Abba," an Aramaic word roughly translated as "Daddy." He pours out his pain and begs for relief. Nonetheless, his determination to do his Father's will is greater than the weight of everything set before him. Time with his Father calms his heart and cements his choice.

Jesus will go to the cross at Golgotha because he went to his knees at Gethsemane.

Perhaps the real moment of truth wasn't in his public execution, but rather in the intimacy of this private prayer. Not in the glaring brightness of noonday, but in the lonely darkness of midnight. For the issue was settled then and there. What follows— though eternally indispensable—is still only the aftermath of his absolute resolve to do the will of his Father.

PRAYER: Jesus, you know what it's like to be overwhelmed to the point of death. Even though you are fully God and fully human, this didn't minimize your pain and suffering. Facing such despair and darkness, help me to pray as you prayed, "Father, not my will but yours be done." Amen.

EPISODE 86

BETRAYED BY A KISS

14:37 Then he returned to his disciples and found them sleeping. "Simon," he said to Peter, "are you asleep? Couldn't you keep watch for one hour? 38 Watch and pray so that you will not fall into temptation. The spirit is willing, but the flesh is weak." 39 Once more he went away and prayed the same thing.

Even as he faces the unimaginable, Jesus invites his inner circle to come alongside him. Well aware of their weaknesses, he still covets their presence and prayers.

40 When he came back, he again found them sleeping, because their eyes were heavy. They did not know what to say to him. 41 Returning the third time, he said to them, "Are you still sleeping and resting? Enough! The hour has come. Look, the Son of Man is delivered into the hands of sinners. 42 Rise! Let us go! Here comes my betrayer!"

The number three has great meaning in Scripture. It's no accident that the disciples fall asleep three times and that Peter denies Christ three times. One time may be an accident. Twice might be a coincidence. But a trinity represents an absolute completeness, an indisputable certainty, an integrated whole.

> *43 Just as he was speaking, Judas, one of the Twelve, appeared. With him was a crowd armed with swords and clubs, sent from the chief priests, the teachers of the law, and the elders. 44 Now the betrayer had arranged a signal with them: "The one I kiss is the man; arrest him and lead him away under guard." 45 Going at once to Jesus, Judas said, "Rabbi!" and kissed him. 46 The men seized Jesus and arrested him.*

This is perhaps the most absurd act in the entire drama of human history: the arrest of God. And it's accomplished by the most tender of human acts: the kiss of a friend.

PRAYER: Lord, how you must have felt that night! Disappointed by your dearest friends, sold out by a close follower, betrayed with a kiss, and then seized by an armed mob. And yet, you plunge into the deadly waters of our redemption with abandon. I am undone in the presence of such love. Amen.

EPISODE 87

FLEEING IN FEAR

14:47 Then one of those standing near drew his sword and struck the servant of the high priest, cutting off his ear. 48 "Am I leading a rebellion," said Jesus, "that you have come out with swords and clubs to capture me? 49 Every day I was with you, teaching in the temple courts, and you did not arrest me. But the Scriptures must be fulfilled."

Jesus exposes their cowardice and treachery, even as he reminds them that their own Scriptures predict these exact circumstances.

50 Then everyone deserted him and fled. 51 A young man, wearing nothing but a linen garment, was following Jesus. When they seized him, 52 he fled naked, leaving his garment behind.

Some scholars believe that the young man who ran away was actually John Mark, the author of this Gospel. How telling that the author doesn't write himself into the story as a hero but rather as a naked coward fleeing for his life.

This is what the gospel does to the human heart. Instead of seeing ourselves in the light of our strengths, we see God's grace in the light of our weaknesses.

Whether or not this young man was Mark, Mark infuses this self-awareness into his description of Peter, his mentor, through whose eyes the story is recounted. Throughout this Gospel, Peter is alternately brash and boisterous or anxious and afraid. He's not the story's hero; rather, Jesus is. After Pentecost, this disciple with feet of clay will be transformed into The Rock—God's steady and sturdy spokesperson.

But for the time being, he and the other disciples flee in fear.

PRAYER: Jesus, thank you for helping me see my own shortcomings in the lives of those you loved most dearly. They failed you and yet you never failed them. They were weak in their own strength but became strong in yours. And while they could never forgive themselves for deserting you, your forgiveness redeemed and restored them, as it does us. Thank you. Amen.

EPISODE 88

A MOCKERY OF JUSTICE

14:53 They took Jesus to the high priest, and all the chief priests, elders and teachers of the law came together.

Jesus is taken before Israel's supreme court, known as the Great Sanhedrin, and Israel's supreme religious leader, the high priest. This is remarkable because their law forbids the convening of this council during a religious observance such as the Passover. It's also remarkable that such a large group—certainly more than a hundred key leaders—has conspired to meet in the middle of the night to deal with Jesus.

54 Peter followed him at a distance, right into the courtyard of the high priest. There he sat with the guards and warmed himself at the fire.

Peter's point of view is especially evident in this passage.

55 The chief priests and the whole Sanhedrin were looking for evidence against Jesus so that they could

*put him to death, but they did not find any. 56 Many
testified falsely against him, but their statements did
not agree.*

The Sanhedrin is Israel's highest ruling council,
traditionally comprised of 71 "sages." On this
occasion, the high priest himself presides over the
assembly. They are joined by other chief priests, elders,
and legal experts who are seeking a legal pretense upon
which to convict and execute Jesus.

*57 Then some stood up and gave this false testimony
against him: 58 "We heard him say, 'I will destroy
this temple made with human hands and in three days
will build another, not made by man.' " 59 Yet even
then their testimony did not agree. 60 Then the high
priest stood up before them and asked Jesus, "Are you
not going to answer? What is this testimony that these
men are bringing against you?"*

In the American justice system, a criminal
defendant is presumed to be innocent and the
prosecution must convince the court of his guilt
beyond a reasonable doubt. The 5th Amendment to
the U.S. Constitution allows the defendant the
privilege of remaining silent, casting the entire burden
of proof upon the accusing party.

At Jesus' trial, the high priest demands that Christ
defend himself against false testimony and conflicting
evidence. But Jesus owes no duty to hypocrites and
liars. His silence must have been infuriating to those
whose every word confirmed their own culpability.

61 But Jesus remained silent and gave no answer. Again the high priest asked him, "Are you the Christ, the Son of the Blessed One?" 62 "I am," said Jesus. "And you will see the Son of Man sitting at the right hand of the Mighty One and coming on the clouds of heaven."

The high priest plays his trump card. If he can get Jesus to commit blasphemy, his case is closed. So he asks Jesus directly if he is the Christ, God's anointed Son. Underlying this question is the assumption that the religious elite of Israel would surely recognize the Messiah if they saw him.

Jesus' simple answer is earth-shaking: *I am.*

As if to underscore his divine Sonship, Jesus uses a phrase that is shorthand for "I Am That I Am," the name that God revealed to Moses in the third chapter of Exodus. Throughout Israel's history, the Jews have trusted "I Am" for deliverance and blessing. Now, Jesus has the impudence to use these words to describe himself.

But his audacity does not end there.

Jesus tells the supreme court of Israel that one day they will all see him revealed as the Messianic Son of God comes in glory *to sit in judgment of them!*

63 The high priest tore his clothes. "Why do we need any more witnesses?" he asked. 64 "You have heard the blasphemy. What do you think?" They all condemned him as worthy of death.

The irony is astounding.

Once a year, on the Day of Atonement, Israel's

high priest may enter the Temple's Holy of Holies on behalf of the Jewish nation to present a blood sacrifice in payment for their sins. The man who has this hallowed responsibility is now passing judgment on the True High Priest—not only of Israel, but of all humanity. Even more, Jesus himself would soon become the blood sacrifice that would atone for the sins of the whole world.

> *65 Then some began to spit at him; they blindfolded him, struck him with their fists, and said, "Prophesy!" And the guards took him and beat him.*

Once the guilty verdict is in, their false civility turns to cruelty. First, they blindfold Jesus so they won't have to look him in the eye. Then they add injury to insult by pummeling him with their fists and clubs. But this is just the beginning of the cruelty to come.

PRAYER: Jesus, it's outrageous that you were condemned to death by the very men for whom you would lay down your life. The highest court in the land convicted the world's only truly innocent man. Thank you for enduring this mockery of justice to make us just in your Father's sight. Amen.

EPISODE 89

THE TRIAL IN THE COURTYARD

14:66 While Peter was below in the courtyard, one of the servant girls of the high priest came by. 67 When she saw Peter warming himself, she looked closely at him. "You also were with that Nazarene, Jesus," she said. 68 But he denied it. "I don't know or understand what you're talking about," he said, and went out into the entryway. 69 When the servant girl saw him there, she said again to those standing around, "This fellow is one of them." 70 Again he denied it. After a little while, those standing near said to Peter, "Surely you are one of them, for you are a Galilean." 71 He began to call down curses, and he swore to them, "I don't know this man you're talking about." 72 Immediately the rooster crowed the second time. Then Peter remembered the word Jesus had spoken to him: "Before the rooster crows twice you will disown me three times." And he broke down and wept.

Even as Israel's highest court wrongly convicts Jesus, another trial is going on in the courtyard below. Peter finds himself rightly accused of following Christ by a lowly servant girl. He condemns himself by his own false testimony.

Only hours earlier, Peter had vowed to die with Christ. But he has just seen the unthinkable: Jesus sentenced to death and then beaten by the taunting mob as he's led away.

Peter is undone.

Cowering in the shadows, the persistent accusations of a servant girl make him lash out in profane denial. As the rooster crows, Peter recalls Jesus' prediction and breaks down in tears. Not the quiet tears that roll off the edges of the eyes but the chest-heaving, gut-wrenching weeping of inconsolable grief. Although dawn is breaking, Peter's world has never been darker.

PRAYER: Jesus, please forgive me when I deny you by thought or by deed. Let my words and actions testify to your lordship in my life. Help me live consistently and gracefully so that all might know your love and mercy. Amen.

MARK 15

EPISODE 90

BROUGHT BEFORE PILATE

15:1 Very early in the morning, the chief priests, with the elders, the teachers of the law and the whole Sanhedrin, made their plans. So they bound Jesus, led him away and handed him over to Pilate.

Even though the Jewish ruling council has condemned Jesus to death, they don't have the civil authority to execute him. This power is held by Pontius Pilate, the Roman governor for the region of Judea. The Jewish leadership has a tenuous relationship with the Roman authorities. They are allowed relative freedom to practice their religion so long as the peace is kept, taxes are collected, and Caesar is honored. Consequently, it's in Pilate's interest to occasionally indulge the wishes of the Sanhedrin. Even if that means holding court at dawn.

2 "Are you the king of the Jews?" asked Pilate. "You have said so," Jesus replied.

The Jewish council knows that Pilate won't execute someone for blasphemy, so they bring Jesus to him on charges of inciting rebellion against the government. Anyone claiming to be king of the Jews and mounting an insurgency would be a clear and present threat to the peace. The last thing that Pilate needs is another Jewish zealot raising the messianic hopes of Israel for deliverance from Rome. But that's not what he finds.

Pilate asks Christ if he is king of the Jews and Jesus quietly agrees. There's no political tirade, no prophetic rant, no castigation of the Jewish leadership and their unholy alliance with the Roman Empire. Just *"Whatever you say."* In fact, Jesus appears so meek and non-threatening that his accusers must redouble their efforts to make him look guilty.

> *3 The chief priests accused him of many things. 4 So again Pilate asked him, "Aren't you going to answer? See how many things they are accusing you of." 5 But Jesus still made no reply, and Pilate was amazed.*

Pilate's astonishment is probably due to two factors. First, he's surprised that someone accused of a capital crime isn't desperately pleading for his life. Likewise, he's astounded these religious leaders are so hell-bent on killing someone who appears so passive. It's obvious to the governor that the Sanhedrin is jealous of Jesus' popularity, so Pilate concocts a back-door plan to release him.

> *6 Now it was the custom at the Feast to release a prisoner whom the people requested. 7 A man called*

Barabbas was in prison with the insurrectionists who had committed murder in the uprising. 8 The crowd came up and asked Pilate to do for them what he usually did. 9 "Do you want me to release to you the king of the Jews?" asked Pilate, 10 knowing it was out of self-interest that the chief priests had handed Jesus over to him. 11 But the chief priests stirred up the crowd to have Pilate release Barabbas instead. 12 "What shall I do, then, with the one you call the king of the Jews?" Pilate asked them.

Clearly, Pilate has the authority to deny the Jewish Council's request to execute Jesus. Instead, he tells the crowd that—to honor their Jewish holiday—he'll pardon either the popular rabbi or a convicted felon. It's their choice.

Ironically, Barabbas is actually guilty of sedition, the same charge that can't be proven against Jesus. To Pilate's surprise, the religious leaders whip the crowd into a bloodthirsty mob crying for Jesus' execution.

13 "Crucify him!" they shouted. 14 "Why? What crime has he committed?" asked Pilate. But they shouted all the louder, "Crucify him!" 15 Wanting to satisfy the crowd, Pilate released Barabbas to them. He had Jesus flogged, and handed him over to be crucified.

Jew and Gentile, clergy and politician, citizen and soldier—each and all are responsible for Jesus' crucifixion. And appropriately, his sacrificial death will be on behalf of the entire world.

PRAYER: Jesus, rather than defending your own life, you allowed yourself to be condemned so that my life might be spared. Men conspired against you--unaware that you, your Father and your Spirit were carrying out an even greater conspiracy to deliver humanity from its own deceit and sin. Thank you, Lord. Amen.

EPISODE 91

MOCKED AND BEATEN

15:16 The soldiers led Jesus away into the palace (that is, the Praetorium) and called together the whole company of soldiers. 17 They put a purple robe on him, then twisted together a crown of thorns and set it on him. 18 And they began to call out to him, "Hail, king of the Jews!" 19 Again and again they struck him on the head with a staff and spit on him. Falling on their knees, they paid homage to him. 20 And when they had mocked him, they took off the purple robe and put his own clothes on him. Then they led him out to crucify him.

The unbridled fury unleashed upon Jesus is a testimony to the decadence of humanity and to the existence of evil. For three years, Jesus has loved the unloved, fed the hungry, healed the sick, freed the demonically oppressed, and raised the dead.

For these offenses, his back is torn open with a leather cat-of-nine tails, a crown of thorns is shoved onto his bleeding head, and he is viciously beaten with a mock scepter as the crowd jeers and curses him.

21 A certain man from Cyrene, Simon, the father of Alexander and Rufus, was passing by on his way in from the country, and they forced him to carry the cross.

Ordinarily, a condemned prisoner bore his cross through the mocking crowds, beyond the city gates, up to the hill where his brutal execution would deter those who might challenge the authority of the Sanhedrin or the supremacy of Caesar. But Jesus has been beaten so severely that he can't carry his cross the whole way. So Simon, a bystander, is pressed into service by the Roman guards escorting Jesus to his death.

Simon was visiting from Cyrene, a Jewish community in the present day northern African country of Libya. The fact that Mark names both of his children may indicate that Alexander and Rufus were well-known and highly regarded by first century believers.

Even as Mark's Gospel approaches its climax, its author takes the time to include the names of eyewitnesses who can confirm the veracity of his story.

PRAYER: Father, that you would allow your Son to be ridiculed, tortured, and eventually executed on my behalf bears witness to your unwavering love for humanity. It's not only what you chose to do that amazes me; it's what you chose not to do. Let my wonder result in obedience and worship. Amen.

EPISODE 92

CRUCIFIXION

15:22 They brought Jesus to the place called Golgotha (which means "the place of the skull"). 23 Then they offered him wine mixed with myrrh, but he did not take it. 24 And they crucified him. Dividing up his clothes, they cast lots to see what each would get.

Golgotha is a craggy mount outside the walls of Jerusalem whose rock face reminds onlookers of the eye and nose sockets of a human skull. Because public executions are performed there, its name carries a double meaning.

As they stretch Christ out on the cross and gather the nails to hammer into his flesh, his executioners offer him wine mixed with an analgesic to dull the pain of his final moments on earth. But Jesus has vowed not to drink of the fruit of the vine again until he does so in his Father's kingdom. So he rejects their offer.

More significantly, Jesus refuses to compromise the acuity of his mind and spirit as he bears the full weight of mankind's sin upon himself. As God's Son, he can stop this atrocity at any instant. But because the whole story of salvation is riding on his willing self-sacrifice, Jesus will not allow anything to impair his judgment or weaken his resolve.

He feels each strike of the hammer as the nails pound through his flesh into the wood beneath. As the cross is erected and dropped into place, every synapse is engulfed in agony. Jesus must push downward against the nails in his feet in order for his chest to press upward for each lungful of air. Crucifixion is the very definition of cruel and unusual punishment.

PRAYER: Jesus, thank you for not cutting any corners on the road to our redemption. You faced this impossible ordeal with a clear mind and a willing heart. What few earthly possessions you owned were taken from you. And yet your sacrifice will purchase back all of humanity. You are worthy of my devotion and praise. Amen.

EPISODE 93

JESUS DIES

15:25 It was nine in the morning when they crucified him. 26 The written notice of the charge against him read: THE KING OF THE JEWS.

It's nine o'clock, Friday morning, and the fate of the whole world is literally hanging on a rough-hewn cross atop a hillside in Israel.

Roman law requires that a criminal's charges be clearly posted for all to see. Pilate, recently outmaneuvered by the Sanhedrin, wants the last word. So he hangs a sign that says "The King of the Jews" above the dying Galilean. The Jewish Council complains that the charges should actually read, "He *claimed* to be the King of the Jews" (John 19:21). But Pilate thumbs his nose at them by refusing to change what has been written.

27 They crucified two robbers with him, one on his right and one on his left. 29 Those who passed by hurled insults at him, shaking their heads and saying, "So! You who are going to destroy the temple and build it in three days, 30 come down from the cross and save yourself!" 31 In the same way the chief priests and the teachers of the law mocked him among themselves. "He saved others," they said, "but he can't save himself! 32 Let this Messiah, this king of Israel, come down now from the cross, that we may see and believe." Those crucified with him also heaped insults on him.

The pain is excruciating; the insults, unrelenting. Christ is jeered by the trustees of the very Law and Prophets he came to fulfill. His own words are twisted and hurled back against him. Even the dying criminals join the tirade, which persists for three solid hours.

33 At noon, darkness came over the whole land until three in the afternoon.

At high noon—¬the sixth hour by the Jewish clock—the sun disappears and the entire country is plunged into blackness.

Imagine the mayhem!

The Jewish nation has seen their God do this before—*but to their enemies!* This is not simply a solar eclipse; the darkness endures three hours.

While Israel's religious and political leaders are reacting to these signs in the heavens, God's Son is redeeming the world.

34 And three in the afternoon Jesus cried out in a loud voice, "Eloi, Eloi, lema sabachthani?"—which means, "My God, my God, why have you forsaken me?"

The last words of Christ were actually uttered a

thousand years earlier by Israel's King David and are recorded in the 22nd Psalm. Far from simply being a despondent cry of abandonment, these verses predict Jesus' crucifixion in breathtaking detail. Even more, Psalm 22 crescendos with an unwavering faith that the Father will deliver him. Although the Jews had sung these lyrics in worship for centuries, those gathered at Golgotha are oblivious to the fact that it's their own mocking words and vicious actions that had been prophesied by David. Scripture was being fulfilled before their own blind eyes.

<u>Psalm 22 (select verses):</u>

1 My God, my God, why have you forsaken me? Why are you so far from saving me, so far from my cries of anguish? 2 My God, I cry out by day, but you do not answer, by night, but I find no rest....

6 But I am a worm and not a man, scorned by men and despised by the people. 7 All who see me mock me; they hurl insults, shaking their heads: 8 "He trusts in the Lord; let the LORD rescue him. Let him deliver him, since he delights in him."

11 Do not be far from me, for trouble is near and there is no one to help....

13 Roaring lions tearing their prey open their mouths wide against me. 14 I am poured out like water, and all my bones are out of joint. My heart has turned to wax; it has melted away within me. 15 My strength is dried up like a potsherd, and my tongue sticks to the roof of my mouth; you lay me in the dust of death. 16 Dogs have surrounded me; a pack of villains encircle me, they have pierced my hands and my feet. 17 All my bones are on display; people stare and gloat over me.18 They divide my clothes among them and cast lots for my garment.19 But you, LORD, do not be far from me. You are my strength; come quickly to help me.

This psalm catalogs the jeering crowds, the flesh-tearing torture, the dislocation of bones from joints, the piercing of his hands and feet, the unquenchable thirst, and the gambling for his garments that would mark the Messiah's crucifixion. What are the odds that a prophecy uttered a thousand years earlier would be fulfilled in such detail?

15:35 When some of those standing near heard this, they said, "Listen, he's calling Elijah." 36 One man ran, filled a sponge with wine vinegar, put it on a stick, and offered it to Jesus to drink. "Now leave him alone. Let's see if Elijah comes to take him down," he said.37 With a loud cry, Jesus breathed his last. 38 The curtain of the temple was torn in two from top to bottom.

It's three o'clock in the afternoon. A pitch-black afternoon. Jesus cries out one last time. And dies.

There are no breaths left to breathe. No lessons left to teach. It is finished. He is spent.

The price has been paid.

In full.

PRAYER: Lord Jesus, nothing that has ever happened or that will ever happen can rival your sacrifice on the Cross. Innumerable prophecies are fulfilled and humanity's debt is paid in full. You exchanged your righteousness for my sin and your life for mine. I can only respond by giving you my life and worship. Amen.

EPISODE 94

THE WITNESS OF WOMEN

15:39 And when the centurion, who stood there in front of Jesus, heard his cry and saw how he died, he said, "Surely this man was the Son of God!"

The kingdom doors have now been flung open to all who will trust the saving work of Christ. As if on cue, the very man who led Jesus to the cross now confesses his divinity.

40 Some women were watching from a distance. Among them were Mary Magdalene, Mary the mother of James the younger and of Joseph, and Salome. 41 In Galilee these women had followed him and cared for his needs. Many other women who had come up with him to Jerusalem were also there.

Jesus' male disciples fear for their safety and have fled the scene. Several women followers, however, risk life and limb to witness Jesus' crucifixion. Mark makes a point to record their names for posterity.

In contrast to the dominant teaching of the day, Jesus doesn't treat women as second-class citizens. He ignores the social prohibition against talking with and teaching women. He demonstrates concern for widows and single mothers. Several women form the core of his support group.

Ironically, the witness of women in that day was often legally inadmissible. Nonetheless, in three days, the resurrected Christ will make his first appearance to women.

Even at his death, Mark shows how revolutionary Jesus' life has been.

PRAYER: Lord, you show no favoritism between male or female, Jew or Gentile, slave or free. In your kingdom, each of us is your favorite. The ground is level at the foot of your cross. Thank you for such infinite and unconditional love. Amen.

EPISODE 95

JOSEPH CLAIMS JESUS' BODY

15:42 It was Preparation Day (that is, the day before the Sabbath). So as evening approached, 43 Joseph of Arimathea, a prominent member of the Council, who was himself waiting for the kingdom of God, went boldly to Pilate and asked for Jesus' body. 44 Pilate was surprised to hear that he was already dead. Summoning the centurion, he asked him if Jesus had already died. 45 When he learned from the centurion that it was so, he gave the body to Joseph.

The Jewish Sabbath begins each Friday at sunset, so only three hours remain until all work must cease. Jewish regulations won't allow a dead body to remain on a cross over the Sabbath, lest the day be desecrated and the land itself defiled. Accordingly, the Roman executioners would ordinarily break the legs of those being crucified to hasten their deaths as sunset approached.

Joseph of Arimathea, a member of the Sanhedrin who is sympathetic to Jesus, defies his colleagues by asking Pilate if he can take responsibility for the body. The governor is skeptical that Jesus has already died, so he asks the captain of the guard to verify this report. The centurion, who must be truthful under penalty of death, confirms that Christ is actually dead. The fact that an objective third party authenticates Jesus' death is critically important, since some of his detractors—then and now—will claim that Jesus merely "swooned" on the cross and later recovered to fake his resurrection from the dead.

No. Jesus is truly dead.

46 So Joseph bought some linen cloth, took down the body, wrapped it in the linen, and placed it in a tomb cut out of rock. Then he rolled a stone against the entrance of the tomb. 47 Mary Magdalene and Mary the mother of Joseph saw where he was laid.

Rather than being dumped in a pauper's grave, Jesus' carefully wrapped corpse is laid in Joseph's prestigious unused stone tomb. Failing to defend Jesus in life, perhaps Joseph can esteem him in death.

As the sun sets on the most important day the world has ever known, it is unaware that an even more titanic event awaits on the other side of the Sabbath.

PRAYER: Sometimes it's difficult for me to comprehend that you truly died. You passed from life to death so that we might pass from death to life. Your body ceased to function and your spirit went to the place of the dead. Once there, you opened the doors of the grave from the inside and led those under the curse into eternal blessing. Thank you for loving the world—and me—so much. Amen.

MARK 16

EPISODE 96

JESUS IS RISEN!

Today, there are more than 150,000 Jewish graves on the Mount of Olives alone, crowded together on this steep hillside overlooking Israel's holy city of Jerusalem. Through the centuries, most Jews have clung fervently to the hope that one day God would raise the righteous from the dead. As such, they believed there's a sacred duty to prepare the bodies of the dead for burial and eventual resurrection. Conversely, Middle Easterners might allow the corpse of a criminal or traitor to be thrown to the dogs or eaten by vultures, believing that this destroyed their hope of an eternal body.

As the sun sets on Good Friday, Joseph of Arimethea intervenes to insure that Jesus' body isn't desecrated. As dawn breaks on Easter Sunday, a small band of women venture into the cemetery where Christ's body is entombed to complete the burial preparations that had been cut short by the Sabbath.

16:1 When the Sabbath was over, Mary Magdalene, Mary the mother of James, and Salome bought spices so that they might go to anoint Jesus' body. 2 Very early on the first day of the week, just after sunrise, they were on their way to the tomb 3 and they asked each other, "Who will roll the stone away from the entrance of the tomb?" 4 But when they looked up, they saw that the stone, which was very large, had been rolled away.

These women had seen Joseph seal Jesus' tomb with a large rock. Now they wonder who will help them move the heavy stone from its entrance. But to their surprise and confusion, they find it's already been rolled away.

5 As they entered the tomb, they saw a young man dressed in a white robe sitting on the right side, and they were alarmed.6 "Don't be alarmed," he said. "You are looking for Jesus the Nazarene, who was crucified. He has risen! He is not here. See the place where they laid him.

Joseph's burial vault is evidently large enough to hold these women and a stranger who is sitting inside on the right. Mark records that the man is dressed in white, indicating that he's a divine messenger. The angel's first words are the same ones recorded in virtually every other biblical encounter between an angel and a mortal: Fear not.

The angel knows that Jesus' friends are worried that his body has suffered some further indignity. So he hopes to comfort and encourage them with an earth-shaking announcement: Christ is risen! See for yourselves! He's not here!

> *7 But go, tell his disciples and Peter, 'He is going ahead of you into Galilee. There you will see him, just as he told you.'" 8 Trembling and bewildered, the women went out and fled from the tomb. They said nothing to anyone, because they were afraid.*

The risen Christ has entrusted this angel with a very specific message for the disciples and for Peter, who has dishonored his Lord by denying and cursing him. The angel reminds them that Jesus—at the Last Supper—clearly said he would be crucified, resurrected, and then would go ahead of them to Galilee.

The tomb is empty. An angel has proclaimed Christ's resurrection. And very shortly, his disciples will see him again.

It's at this point that the earliest manuscripts of Mark's Gospel end.

PRAYER: Lord, even though you tell us things time and again, we find ourselves fearfully trusting our senses instead of faithfully trusting your Word. Free us to hear you, believe you, and follow you. For what you have in mind for us is so much greater than we can comprehend. Amen.

EPISODE 97

EPILOGUE

16:9 When Jesus rose early on the first day of the week, he appeared first to Mary Magdalene, out of whom he had driven seven demons.10 She went and told those who had been with him and who were mourning and weeping. 11 When they heard that Jesus was alive and that she had seen him, they did not believe it.

The most reliable manuscripts of Mark (as well as other ancient sources) don't include verses 9 through 20, but most Bibles publish these additional verses because their content is clearly consistent with the other Gospels and New Testament letters.

Why does Mark's Gospel end without a clear sense of closure?

Perhaps John Mark has simply finished writing.

Or perhaps he meant for his biography to dovetail with other written accounts of the resurrected Christ, the birth of the church at Pentecost, and the spread of Christianity across the known world. Certainly, the "rest of the story" can be found in other New Testament accounts.

Mark's Gospel has already recorded that Mary

Magdalene is among the women who found the stone rolled away and the tomb empty. In John's Gospel, Mary leaves the tomb to find Peter and John, who accompany her back to investigate for themselves. John records that Mary is still under the impression that Jesus' body has been moved and shares her anguish with someone she believes to be the cemetery groundskeeper, only to look up and discover she's actually speaking to Jesus. All four Gospels record that there's a great deal of initial skepticism and confusion about Jesus' resurrection that subsides as more and more people actually see Christ.

Whatever the reason, this 12-verse epilogue efficiently sums up the period between Easter Sunday and Jesus' ascension and sets the stage for the explosive evangelistic movement that would eventually spread the Gospel to the ends of the earth.

PRAYER: Our Father in Heaven, thank you for including everything in Scripture that we need to know. Let me dig even deeper into your Word so that your Holy Spirit can transform the deepest places of my heart. Amen.

EPISODE 98

CONVINCING APPEARANCES

16:12 Afterward Jesus appeared in a different form to two of them while they were walking in the country. 13 These returned and reported it to the rest; but they did not believe them either.

This particular encounter is also recorded in Luke 24:13-35 and involves two disciples walking on the road to the village of Emmaus. They are joined by a third man who reveals himself as Christ after explaining how prophecy after prophecy was fulfilled in the circumstances of his death and resurrection.

14 Later Jesus appeared to the Eleven as they were eating; he rebuked them for their lack of faith and their stubborn refusal to believe those who had seen him after he had risen.

In Luke 24:36-49, Jesus miraculously appears to the Eleven to convince them that he has indeed risen from the dead. John 20:19-29 details two separate incidents where Christ actually materializes within locked rooms to demonstrate that he's alive. All told, the New Testament records that Jesus appeared to more than 500 witnesses before returning to heaven (1 Corinthians 15:6).

The resurrection is a reality.

A man who was brutally tortured and executed has been raised from the dead. But there is more to the story. The real miracle is that the Son of God stepped into our shoes to bear the penalty for our crimes against God.

To a man, each of the Eleven, though initially skeptical, will pour out their lives testifying about their risen Lord.

PRAYER: Jesus, purge any lingering skepticism in my heart. Replace the tyranny of doubt with the freedom of faith. Let my witness be compelling in both word and deed so that my life may be a living testimony to your glory. Amen.

EPISODE 99

GO TELL THE WORLD

16:15 He said to them, "Go into all the world and preach the good news to all creation. 16 Whoever believes and is baptized will be saved, but whoever does not believe will be condemned.

This passage, often referred to as "The Great Commission," is echoed in both Luke and Matthew—although the latter version (Matt. 28:18-20) is more extensive and more frequently quoted. All three synoptic gospels contain Christ's command to communicate the good news of God's forgiveness and redemption to a world that would be lost without it.

17 And these signs will accompany those who believe: In my name they will drive out demons; they will speak in new tongues; 18 they will pick up snakes with their hands; and when they drink deadly poison, it will not hurt them at all; they will place their hands on sick people, and they will get well."

This promise that these signs and wonders will accompany those who believe isn't specifically found elsewhere in the Gospels. However, these types of miracles characterized the expansion of the first century church and are chronicled by Luke in the book of Acts. Even today, in the Third World, missionaries attest to innumerable miraculous signs and wonders that draw people's hearts to the gospel message.

In more modern cultures, there are certainly other kinds of signs that point people to Christ. Individuals delivered from physical, spiritual, and emotional affliction. Restored families. Recovering addicts. Sacrificial giving. Selfless service to the poor, sick and disenfranchised. In one sense, these kinds of signs are even more compelling than raising the dead—because they involve the transformation of the human heart.

What's at stake is nothing less than the destiny of people—both near and far off. If our lives point others to Christ, people will have the opportunity to know God's life-changing mercy and grace. If our witness is impotent and unconvincing, then we've missed an opportunity for others to experience the kingdom of God—for now and perhaps for eternity.

Jesus has the audacity to make us his spokespersons. He promises to give us the words and the power to speak them, but we must be willing ambassadors of his Father's kingdom.

PRAYER: Lord, you told us that signs would accompany those who believe. Make my life a sign that points clearly to you and your love, mercy and grace. Give me a joyful burden to pray for and witness to specific people in my world. Amen.

EPISODE 100

JESUS RETURNS TO HEAVEN

16:19 After the Lord Jesus had spoken to them, he was taken up into heaven and he sat at the right hand of God. 20 Then the disciples went out and preached everywhere, and the Lord worked with them and confirmed his word by the signs that accompanied it.

How indescribable this event must have been! The resurrected Christ—who has appeared to hundreds of his followers over the past 40 days—now ascends to his place of honor and authority at his Father's side. The conventional sense that heaven is "up" is certainly more figurative than literal, but it conveys the supremacy and majesty of God's dwelling place.

Luke also records the ascension of Jesus at the end of his Gospel (Luke 24:50-51) as well as in the prologue of the Book of Acts (Acts 1:1-11).

This passage concludes by proclaiming that the Lord's Spirit worked through his disciples to accomplish the Great Commission he had given them. The Good News that Mark heralds in the first chapter of his Gospel is now being amplified to the whole world by the end of his story.

Jesus' ascension puts to rest any possible doubts about his divinity. He reclaims the throne he abandoned on our behalf. He returns to heaven as both Son of Man and Son of God—championing our prayers and guarding our hearts until he returns again to inaugurate a new heaven and new earth.

In this sense, while the end of the story is known, there is still much to be written.

PRAYER: Heavenly Father, thank you for sending your Son to purchase me a place in your story. Thank you for sending your Spirit to empower me to be your faithful witness. Make me an instrument of your peace in this world until your kingdom comes in fullness. In Jesus' Name I pray. Amen.

POSTSCRIPT

If all I knew about Christ were found in Mark's Gospel, here's what I would know:

• Jesus clearly understands himself to be the world's Savior, sent by God to die a sacrificial death that will redeem us from our sins and give us eternal life.

• Jesus fulfills extensive Jewish prophecy concerning the Messiah and repeatedly predicts his own betrayal, crucifixion, and resurrection.

• Jesus has supernatural knowledge of current and future events, and he shares critical details with his followers.

• Jesus demonstrates his lordship over the natural world by healing physical diseases, miraculously feeding thousands, walking on water, calming a raging storm, and raising the dead.

• Jesus releases men, women, and children from the demonic spiritual forces that possess, oppress, and torment them.

• Jesus is intolerant of religious hypocrisy and religious traditions that misrepresent his Father's love and oppress humanity.

- Jesus shows compassion to the poor, the sick, and the socially unacceptable while challenging the rich, the self-satisfied, and the powerful.

- Jesus tells his followers that their devotion to him is expressed by how they serve others, especially the helpless and hopeless.

- Jesus loves children.

- Jesus' life is saturated with Scripture and prayerful conversation with his heavenly Father.

- Jesus illustrates kingdom principles through stories and parables rather than through a systematic theology.

- Jesus invites his friends into the most intimate moments of his life, looking beyond their weaknesses to the unique potential that will be realized in each of them.

- Jesus teaches that he will return to judge the living and the dead, and he will reign over a new heaven and earth characterized by his Father's power and love.

- Jesus is a person of compassionate action who expects no less of his disciples.

These profound claims can change the trajectory of our lives and our world.

As I stated at the outset, Mark systematically presents witness after witness and evidence after evidence to make the case that Jesus is the Messiah, God's chosen Christ, who will lay down his life for the sins of the world and then be raised from death to demonstrate his sovereignty over life and death itself.

As a trained and licensed attorney, I am familiar with the presentation of evidence in a legal proceeding. Near the end of a jury trial, the judge will "charge" the jury with the responsibility of weighing all the evidence, applying the law to those facts, and then rendering a verdict.

In a very real sense, this is what everyone who reads Mark's Gospel must do. We must reach a verdict from a fact set that leaves us only a handful of choices:

1. First, we could dismiss the entire narrative as outright fiction or myth.

We might concede that the story embodies some transcendent truth but argue that it has no real basis in fact: the whole story is either patently false or hopelessly fanciful.

The problem with this interpretation of Mark is that there are significant and reliable third party accounts of Jesus' life and death written within years of the events themselves. Given the weight of the evidence, it's far more problematic to reject the historical existence of Jesus than to admit that he walked upon the earth.

But if we admit Jesus' existence, then we're stuck with the problem of determining who he was and if his claims of divinity were true.

2. This presents a second alternative: admitting

that Jesus lived but denying he was supernatural.

That's exactly what Thomas Jefferson did. He created his own version of the Bible by taking a razor blade to the Gospel accounts of Matthew, Mark, Luke, and John and cutting out any references to Jesus' miracles or resurrection.

The problem with this approach is that you end up with an entirely different story than the one its writers told. Though all four Gospel authors portray Jesus as an extraordinary man, their unwavering goal is to present him as the unique Son of God whose death and resurrection would redeem the world. To them, he's more than just a sage; he's the Savior. There's simply no way to remove the supernatural elements from the narrative without destroying the whole thing. You can't just "cherry pick" the parts you're willing to believe and dismiss everything else. To do so is not only intellectually dishonest, it's also patronizing to the Gospel writers who ended up authenticating their words with their own blood.

When a witness takes the stand in court, the jury must determine whether or not that witness is reliable. If the jury finds the witness reliable, then it must accept his or her testimony as reliable. The jury is not free to agree or disagree with the testimony; rather, it must accept or reject the witness. This is the same standard we must apply when we consider the witness of the Gospel writers. You and I weren't witnesses to the actual events nor did we carefully interview those who were (Luke 1:1-4). So we are biased jurors if we reject *their testimony* on the basis of *our experience*. Rather, we must weigh their testimony on the basis of *their credibility*. Did several reliable witnesses corroborate the story? Does their testimony stand the test of time? Did the witnesses eventually recant their testimony?

And that's not to say that reliable witnesses can't offer differing testimonies about the details of the events in question. But that doesn't invalidate the fact that certain things actually happened. So while apparent discrepancies may be found in the details of the four Gospels, the central facts of Jesus' miraculous life, death, resurrection, and ascension are undisputed by all four Gospel writers. The early church had no problem embracing any of these ambiguities in light of the overwhelming consistency of the story. The totality of the testimony was persuasive.

If we, as jurors, decide to reject the testimony of reliable witnesses, it's because our own biases and prejudices cause us to do so. If we approach a story about God and miracles with a bias against God and miracles, then we've already pre-judged the narrative. We lack the objectivity required to render an impartial verdict.

It's helpful for us skeptics to remember that none of the Gospel writers were initially inclined to believe this story. Most of them were ardent Jews for whom the idea of the Godhead manifesting itself in human form was blasphemous. Indeed, throughout the Gospels, the writers take great pains to tell how confused and conflicted Jesus' disciples were—until they experienced the resurrected Christ and everything started to make sense. These events were just as unbelievable to those in the first century as they are to people in the twenty-first century.

3. The third option is to accept Mark's testimony about Jesus' life and purpose and to be transformed by faith in Christ.

Even though the arguments and evidence for Christ are compelling, trusting the testimony of the Gospels will eventually require a leap of faith—for the ultimate goal of the Gospels is that we might know Christ himself.

Mark's endgame is that we would one day say what his mentor, Peter, says to Jesus in Mark 8:29: *"You are the Messiah."* Or, as John, his fellow evangelist concludes in his Gospel: *"But these are written that you may believe that Jesus is the Messiah, the Son of God, and that by believing you may have life in his name* (John 20:31)." The purpose of Mark's Gospel is not to get us to agree with its content, but rather for us to believe in its protagonist.

Trusting in the person and work of Christ will change everything.

Instead of seeing life as having a random beginning and a tragic end, we'll begin to see ourselves as being created and redeemed for eternal life with God and our fellow brothers and sisters.

Rather than seeing history in terms of chance and evolution, we'll begin to see the story arc of God's creation, redemption, and restoration of all things. We'll respond to his call to play an active role in his coming kingdom. Rather than continuing to live self-serving and despairing lives, we'll find ourselves deeply transformed by his Spirit to live lives of faith, hope, and love—becoming living witnesses to the gospel that Christ is writing upon our hearts.

275

4.   There is also a fourth (and far too common) option: to tacitly agree with the claims of Christ while living indifferently to them.

Throughout the Bible, we read about people who knew the truth but chose to live in defiance of it. They were either unconsciously deluded or consciously disobedient. I admit I've been both.

In reality, it's folly to embrace the teachings of Christ without accepting the claims of Christ. For Jesus not only maintained that we ought to love God and our neighbor, he also insisted that the only way for us to really do so was *for him to do it on our behalf.* There is no middle ground, we have either set ourselves against him or we have accepted his invitation to be redeemed and transformed by him.

Even today, there are people who claim the name "Christian" while living lives undifferentiated from the rest of the world. These people are *nominal* (lit. "in name only") Christians. Their hypocrisy only serves to tarnish the reputation of Christ and his body, the Church. Nominal Christians might never darken the door of a sanctuary or they might serve in the highest ranks of denominational leadership. In fact, Jesus said that it was possible for false disciples to delude themselves into thinking they were godly because they did all kinds of spiritual things in his name (Matthew 7:21-23).

Perhaps they grew up in a "Christian" home or live in a "Christian" country or claim "Christian" values. But being a true Christ-follower is not a matter of ancestry or nationality or philosophy. Rather, it's about understanding that we are so fallen and broken that the Son of God had to step down into the flesh he created and bear our sins and punishment himself. We are saved by his totally unmerited sacrifice on our behalf. This is called *grace*. The only prerequisite for receiving this free gift is for us to confess our desperate need and trust his complete provision on our behalf. That's why salvation should create a profound sense of humility and gratitude in the lives of believers. We are forgiven to forgive, loved to love, served to serve, and blessed to bless.

As in Jesus day, it's entirely possible to be the most religious person in the room and yet be as lost as the worst sinner in the world. Likewise, it's possible for Jesus to tell the world's worst person, *"Truly I tell you, today you will be with me in paradise"* (Luke 23:43).

The word "Christian" finds its fullest meaning as a noun, not as an adjective. We are Christians (noun) because Christ has redeemed us, not because we ascribe to a Christian (adjective) worldview or listen to Christian (adjective) radio or buy Christian (adjective) books and music. Those who call themselves Christians without being transformed by Christ are like salt that lacks saltiness—good for nothing except to be thrown out and trampled under foot (Matthew 5:13). Or like a fruit tree that's incapable of bearing fruit—fit only to be cut down and used as kindling (Matthew 7:19).

In a sense, being a nominal Christian is far more dangerous than being a skeptic or non-believer because we've only inoculated ourselves against the true work God wants to do in our lives. We have just enough religion to prevent us from truly dying to self and being born anew in Christ.

I can relate. I grew up in "the church" and made a public profession of my faith in Christ when I was ten. But it wasn't until I was in my teens that I experienced the Holy Spirit challenging my nominal faith and calling me beyond the "lip-service" Christianity with which I'd become so comfortable.

If you're a skeptic who has been turned off by people who hold themselves out as Christians but bear little resemblance to the Christ of Mark's Gospel, I sincerely apologize. But Jesus warned us that this would be the case. That said, I hope that you know sincere, compassionate Christ-followers whose lives are beautifully persuasive.

In closing, ladies and gentlemen of the jury, I encourage you to examine the compelling evidence and credible testimonies presented by John Mark and arrive at the same verdict he did: that Jesus is the Christ, the Son of God, sent to ransom each of us into his Father's eternal Kingdom.

ABOUT THE AUTHOR

Vince Wilcox holds a Bachelor of Arts in Religious Studies (Distinguished Major) from the University of Virginia, a Masters of Science in Education (Guidance & Counseling) from Old Dominion University, and a Doctor of Jurisprudence degree from Nashville School of Law.

He's a licensed attorney in the State of Tennessee, an instructor at Trevecca Nazarene University, and general manager of DiscoverWorship.com. Vince lives with his wife and extended family in Franklin, TN along with their beloved dogs.

In addition to this book, he's written **"The Lord's Prayer: A Verse-By-Verse Devotional Journey"** which is available in Kindle and paperback formats at Amazon.com.

For more, go to vincewilcox.com

© 2018 Vince Wilcox

Made in United States
Troutdale, OR
03/15/2025

29786404R00166